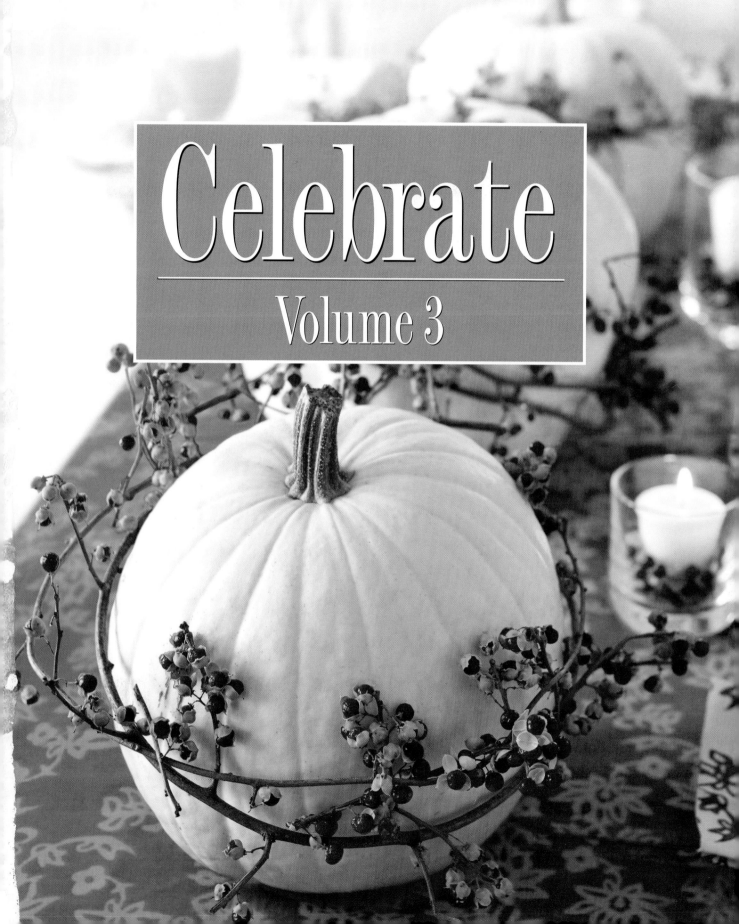

Better Homes and Gardens®

Celebrate

Volume 3

contents

begin

spring

food

Celebrate
Volume 3

MEREDITH CORPORATION CONSUMER MARKETING
Vice President, Consumer Marketing: Janet Donnelly
Consumer Product Marketing Director: Heather Sorensen
Business Director: Ron Clingman
Consumer Marketing Product Manager: Mary Ripperger
Senior Production Manager: Al Rodruck

WATERBURY PUBLICATIONS, INC.
Contributing Editors: Sue Banker, Lois White
Contributing Art Director: Cathy Brett
Contributing Copy Editor: Peg Smith
Contributing Proofreader: Linda Wagner

Editorial Director: Lisa Kingsley
Creative Director: Ken Carlson
Associate Editors: Tricia Bergman, Mary Williams
Associate Design Director: Doug Samuelson
Production Assistant: Mindy Samuelson

BETTER HOMES AND GARDENS MAGAZINE
Editor in Chief: Gayle Goodson Butler
Executive Editor: Oma Blaise Ford
Managing Editor: Greg H. Kayko
Creative Director: Michael D. Belknap
Deputy Editor, Food and Entertaining: Nancy Wall Hopkins

MEREDITH NATIONAL MEDIA GROUP
President: Tom Harty

MEREDITH CORPORATION
Chairman and Chief Executive Officer: Stephen M. Lacy

In Memoriam: E. T. Meredith III (1933–2003)

it's your turn

My grandparents had it—that uncanny ability to transform an ordinary moment into the extraordinary. Whether it was the way my grandma dressed up the dinner table or how my grandpa turned a rainy afternoon into the crafting event of a lifetime, their creative juices flowed 24/7.

What I remember most about those magical moments is how it shaped our relationship. We talked, laughed, and shared our lives with each other. We became closer because of those special times.

Now it's my turn, and yours, to offer the extraordinary to our own family and friends. That's where *Better Homes and Gardens Celebrate* steps in.

Whether you're looking for a special centerpiece idea or a fully dressed table, *Celebrate* offers dozens of ideas for holidays and every day. Surprise your loved ones with these awesome make-it-yourself crafts, or have them join in the fun. Either way, they'll appreciate your special creativity and thoughtfulness.

Maybe you'd like to update meal time. Beginning on page 64, you'll find scrumptious recipes to master in short time. From appetizers to desserts, your family will think you're the most amazing cook around. Don't be surprised when they linger around the dinner table a little longer—what a blessing in disguise. Also, be sure to check out the imaginative foods on pages 130–135 for your next spooky Halloween gathering.

Because we all seem to have more to do these days, what's really great about *Celebrate* is that it offers lots of inspiring ideas that are easy on time. And many of the ideas are transferable. Check out the Easter story on pages 32–35. Many of the floral projects would be just as beautiful to celebrate a birthday or host a shower.

Get ready to make ordinary moments extraordinary. What a perfect way to show your love.

All the best,

Sue Barker

Let the Year begin

A new year offers new beginnings. Make the most of your home and special occasions with inspirational decorating and celebrating that will long be remembered.

Tiered Treasures

Perfect for wrapping small gifts, round papier-mâché boxes stack to appear as a tiered cake. Using birthday wrapping paper or scrapbook paper, cover box bottoms. Cover the lids with coordinating papers, using glue stick or double-sided tape to secure. Poke cake-size candleholders into the lid of the top box, hot-gluing to secure. Press candles into the holders (do not light). Place gifts in each box and stack.

Cake All Around

Extend happy birthday wishes with a tiered "cake" and fanciful greeting card.

Sweet Wishes

Cupcakes are all the rage, and this dimensional one deserves to be delivered in person. To mail it instead, enclose it in an oversized padded envelope and ask that it be hand-stamped.

WHAT YOU'LL NEED

tracing paper; pencil; scissors
polka-dot, bright pink, green print, and brown papers
2×6-inch rectangle birthday print paper
6¼×9½-inch rectangle brown paper with white backing or with white paper cut to fit inside card; glue stick
5½×4-inch rectangle pink striped paper
5¾×4¼-inch rectangle white paper
double-sided tape

WHAT YOU DO

1. Trace the cupcake top, cherry, leaf, and stem patterns on page 154. Use the patterns to cut the shapes from paper.
2. For the bake cup, accordion-fold the length of the 2×6-inch rectangle of birthday print, pleating approximately every ¼ inch.
3. Fold the brown paper in half, narrow sides together. Use glue stick to adhere the white and pink rectangles to the card front.
4. Using the photo as a guide for placement, adhere the cupcake top and cherry to the card front. Place double-sided tape along each end of pleated paper. Angle out the sides and place below cupcake top as shown. Tuck a piece of tape under the bottom to hold bake cup in place.

Football Frenzy

For your next indoor football gathering,
set the game-day mood by displaying your
favorite team colors.

Good Call Container

Whether using for serving pieces or as take-home
favors, black-and-white striped take-out containers
are officially a good idea. For miniature pom-poms,
tie on fringed hair ties in each guest's favorite team
colors to box handles. If you can't find the right
colors, replace the fun addition with several strands
of curling ribbon. To keep unwrapped goodies fresh,
line boxes with clear cellophane bags, available with
food decorating supplies in crafts stores. Use a wire
twist or piece of ribbon to close the bag.

Two-Tone Coaster

Let guests rest their beverage glasses on coasters that cheer on the
team. For each coaster, cut a 5-inch square from heavy cardboard.
From faux leather in two team colors, cut a 1½×5½-inch strip and a
3×5½-inch strip from Color A. From Color B cut a 1½×5½-inch strip.
Zigzag machine-stitch a Color A strip to each side of the Color B
strip. Center the stitched square on top of the cardboard square.
Fold excess fabric to back of cardboard; hot-glue in place, clipping
corners first if needed. Hot-glue covered square to heavy felt; trim
narrow border using pinking shears. To signify team name, apply a
contrasting stitched adhesive monogram on the center stripe.

Scoring Centerpiece

Choose faux leather in team colors to wrap a vase. Measure vase diameter and height. Cut a piece from each leather color one-half the diameter by the height. Zigzag machine-stitch pieces together along two narrow ends. On both opposite ends, affix seven evenly spaced eyelets (approximately ½ inch from edge). Wrap the faux leather piece around the vase, lace eyelets with a new white shoelace, then tie at the top.

Sweet Wraps

Any Valentine will love finding these sweet little somethings waiting where they are least expected.

Candy Box Topper

Create an everlasting mini bouquet to make boxed candies extra special. Group silk flowers and tie with a wide satin ribbon bow. Hot-glue the arrangement to the box top.

Sundae Best

Miniature sundae glasses, available where party accessories are sold, are just the right size to hold a few sweet treats. Use small clear plastic goodie bags to hold a handful of candies then tie the top with a ribbon bow. Nest the bag in a plastic sundae glass so the gift stands upright.

Wrapped Delight

A gift-wrapped surprise is always fun to get, and one decorated with ribbon, a sprig of artificial flowers, and a coordinating sticker is destined to make an everlasting impression.

Pretty and Petite

No need to fire up the oven to use decorative miniature muffin liners. Layer two or three for sturdiness then fill with bite-size candies. Center the bundle on a white tulle circle (available where wedding craft supplies are sold), gather at the top, and tie snugly with a ribbon bow.

Heartfelt Dining

For Your Sweetheart

Does your sweetie like breakfast in bed or a special dinner served on a TV tray so you can watch a movie together? Create the setting with a pink or red color theme, choosing linens, plates, and flowers in a coordinating color. Personalize the place mat by folding a center pleat in a fabric napkin. Press on an adhesive gemmed letter near the front edge. To decorate the place setting, tape a heart-shape cookie cutter to white paper; trim around the edge using decorative-edge scissors. Fill the heart with candy. Use the pattern on page 154 to cut a banner from white paper. Back it with pink paper then trim a narrow border. Write a message on the banner and lay it on the candy-filled heart.

Make any meal as romantic as Valentine's Day dinner with place settings that serve at the dining room table as well as on a TV tray.

Tied and True

Foot-long pieces of red and blue layered ribbons are striking wrapped around a solid white fabric napkin. Hold it in place with a political button poked through all layers of ribbon.

Poking Fun
A miniature flag and sturdy plastic straws adorned with buttons make for fun Presidents' Day additions to a potted plant or floral arrangement.

Banner Buttons

Political buttons are fun to collect and readily available at antiques stores. Use these miniature snippets of history to celebrate Presidents' Day in patriotic style.

Striped Sensation

Transform a plain red pillow into a patriotic beauty. Evenly space and hand-tack three white ribbons and one with a metallic gold design across the pillow top. Affix political buttons on the decorative ribbon.

All Buttoned Up

A gift of popcorn or candies in red, white, and blue deserves special presentation. Cover a papier-mâché cone in red velvet-embossed scrapbook paper and trim the top with wide velvet rickrack. Hot-glue the paper and trim to the cone along with a trim of similar size buttons. Use a plastic treat bag to hold the snack then tie with gold-color cord.

Vintage Appeal

With one poke into the wax, this presidential pin changes a candle into a Presidents' Day centerpiece. Layered ribbons and the striped candle gives it patriotic charm.

Stand Up Straight

Display some large buttons on stands shaped from paper clips. Bend clips into L shapes and tape one onto each button back to stand upright. If desired, edge buttons with cording and affix a ribbon bow to one side.

Clover Power

Celebrate St. Patrick's Day by lavishly spreading the green.

Lollipop Cups

Not even a leprechaun would guess that the bases of these treat cups are clean aerosol spray can lids. Wedge plastic foam into the bottom to enable lollipops to stand. Wrap the lid in a strip of green patterned paper and glue in place using a low-temp glue gun. Glue trim around the top and a dimensional sticker on the front. Stuff the trimmed cup with paper shred, add a few candies, and poke a lollipop in the center.

Cute Cakes

Make cupcakes a wee bit more fun for St. Patrick's Day with green paper liners, frosting, and sprinkles. To make quick toppers, tape a scrapbooking sticker onto a toothpick and poke into the cupcake.

Beribboned Bow

Serve up sweets in a green dish decked out with a green metallic ribbon bow affixed to one side. Use a glue dot to attach a scrapbook sticker to the bow center.

Sweet Stacks

Individually wrapped mints, conveniently in shiny green papers, make adorable favors. Stack mints and hold together with paper strips taped together at the ends. Trim tops with narrow silver paper strips and sparkly clover stickers.

Nibbles and Nominees

Bring glamour to the stage with a black, white, red, and metallic gold color scheme. Arrange foods and favors on all sides of the table to encourage guests to navigate around the enchanting display.

Take-Home Trophies

Award each guest with a favor box brimming with decadent delights. Spray-paint round papier-mâché boxes gold then wrap with wide matching ribbon. Top each box with a gold-painted art manikin and ribbon bow hot-glued in place.

The Winner Is...

Throw a Hollywood-style party in honor of that special red-carpet event. From the moment guests arrive they'll feel like true celebrities.

Picture This

Create a star-studded tabletop, with dozens of overlapping black and white images of celebrity nominees and favorites displayed under a clear acrylic sheet. To highlight films, actresses, and actors, spray frames with red or metallic gold paint and place them strategically around the table.

Formal Affair

Amp up the glam effect with a red netting table runner weighted with shiny high heels. Use your own or spray-paint pairs from secondhand shops.

Color Appeal

Miniature high heels, available as wedding favors at crafts supply stores, are fitting for the occasion when spray painted bright red and filled with lipstick. To trim the toes, press on a layer of gems. Let your high-heeled guests pick their favorite lipstick hue to take home.

VIP Entrance

Partygoers won't mind posing for the paparazzi as they strut down a red fabric-covered walkway. For the finishing touch, use curtain rods with scroll-style finials as posts from which to string metallic gold rope. At the top of each rod, tie a generous red satin bow and adorn with an artificial gold rose.

All That Glitters

Make champagne glasses shimmer even more with adhesive gem clusters. Tie a sheer gold ribbon at the base of each glass for added elegance.

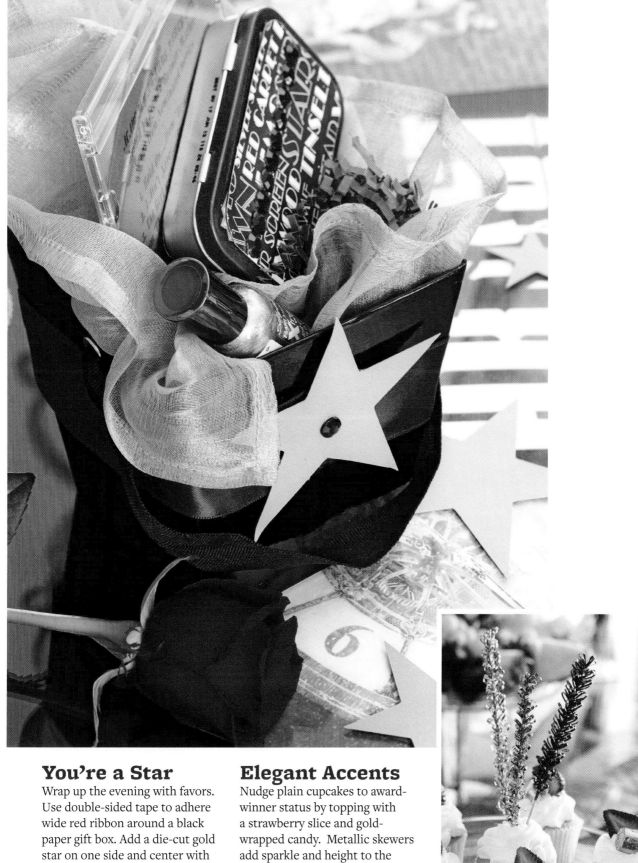

You're a Star

Wrap up the evening with favors. Use double-sided tape to adhere wide red ribbon around a black paper gift box. Add a die-cut gold star on one side and center with a red adhesive gem. Line the box with gold fabric and place small gifts, such as metallic gold nail polish, a paper-covered mint box, and a copy of music from the year's best-loved films.

Elegant Accents

Nudge plain cupcakes to award-winner status by topping with a strawberry slice and gold-wrapped candy. Metallic skewers add sparkle and height to the arrangement.

Easy Does It
love notes

▲ Sweet Sentiments

Use color-coordinated scrapbook trims to frame a picture of your Valentine. Cut or use a pre-made mat and back with decorative paper. A variety of stickers, letters, and ribbons add dimensional detail.

Key to My Heart ▶

Slip your sweetie a note on a card you create. Choose lock- and key-theme stickers to trim a folded scrapbook-paper notecard. To make pieces dimensional, use glue dots to raise cutouts from the background.

Love Tags

Share the symbol of the season—hearts—with those you love. Use the tag patterns on page 154 to cut shapes from Valentine-theme paper. Back each cutout with solid paper and trim as shown. Punch holes in each tag and thread with ball chain.

▼ Message in a Bottle

Write an endearing message on decorative paper and roll it. Place the note in a small bottle (available in crafts and cooking stores) then seal with a cork. Tie a pair of ribbons around the bottle neck.

Apple of ▶ My Eye

A fun lunch box surprise, this apple shines with a message of love. Carefully shape a metal label holder to fit around an apple. Use small adhesive letters to spell "LOVE YOU" on paper to fit holder; tape in place on the back. Thread string through the holes in the label holder and tie around apple.

spring

Throw open the windows and let in the fresh air. Make your home a happy gathering spot, a family refuge, a personal exclamation—it's spring!

Easter Bunny

Blooming Beauty

With a bright cheery palette and flowers freshly picked and arranged, this dining table thrills all. Stagger the height of elements to lend interest. Lots of crisp white on the table allows the colors to pop.

Surprise Pails

Small decorative pails work well to hold personal bouquets for each guest to take home. If pails are not waterproof, line with plastic cups, add water, then fill with fresh daisies. Nestle a colored egg in the center.

Dressed for the Occasion

Invite a pair of white ceramic bunnies to the table. To dress them for the scene, tie ribbon bows around each bunny. Attach two pressed paper flowers together with a brad and hot-glue them to bow centers.

Brunch Welcome Easter morning with a table fashioned for spring.

Bright Spot

No need to purchase Easter dishes when paper brings holiday motifs to the table at a fraction of the price. Top the paper version with a clear glass plate to nudge the place setting from casual to Sunday best. For a quick napkin ring, tie a ribbon bow around a napkin and hot-glue a foil-wrapped Easter candy to the center. For the crowning element, craft an egg-cup candy holder from a pull-apart plastic egg. Separate the halves and hot-glue the rounded ends together using a low-temp glue gun. To help the sections stand securely, sandwich a small washer between the halves. To weight the bottom, glue a fender washer, slightly larger than the small egg half, to the bottom. Give the candy holder a shiny top coat using metallic silver spray paint.

Flower Power

Give place cards a floral facelift by attaching pressed paper flowers to white card stock using colorful brads. To make confetti to sprinkle throughout the table arrangement, punch flower shapes from card stock. Use buttons to accent flowers, hot-gluing them in place.

Teapot Centerpiece

Add height to the table by stacking a teapot atop a pedestal serving piece. Place a vibrant bouquet in the teapot and surround the base with colored eggs.

Artful Baskets

Use baskets creatively to provide lovely holders for nature's vibrant flowers.

Wire Attire
A vintage wire basket lined with moss holds vibrant pansies and nemesia.

Nesting In

This twiggy centerpiece—a basket with a wreath wired on top—gives the look of a bird's nest without disturbing nature. Instead of eggs, fill the center with roses and ferns arranged in water-soaked floral foam and moss.

Flying Colors

Create a hanging basket by attaching a hook and chain to the handle of a wire basket. Use coconut fiber liner and fill with fresh potting mix blended with slow-release fertilizer.

Spring Lineup

Sometimes it works best to keep plants potted separately while grouping them as one. Find a long narrow basket that fits several terra-cotta pots. Line them up in the basket, adding an artificial nest for a darling effect.

May Day Fun

Spread cheer with cleverly packaged confections.

Petal Power
Form flower-like favors by nesting mini paper baking cups inside standard ones. Perch each on an egg cup and fill with colorful nibbles.

Knob Fob

Cone-style cups dressed up with pretty papers and bows make for quick May Day treat holders. To trim wrapped suckers, snip around the edges of paper circles and poke suckers through centers.

Flower Garden

A group of tiny flowerpots makes an unforgettable May Day surprise. Turn to crafts stores to find miniature terra-cotta pots. For each pot, hot-glue a ribbon band to the rim, wedge a piece of plastic foam in the bottom, and cover with paper shred. Poke a toothpick into a foil-wrapped chocolate flower and "plant" in the foam. For large flowerpots, tuck a pair of candy sticks behind the blooms.

Mini Basket

Along with the cupcake rage comes a myriad of crafty liners. Choose one with a deep lip, punch two holes opposite each other, and attach a chenille stem handle, curling at the ends to hold in place. Fill the mini baskets with a sweet and salty mix of popcorn and Easter candies.

Bucket of Fun

A clear miniature plastic pail lets colorful candies show through. To make the container a bit more special, cut a two-layer band of paper to tape around the outside and tie a ribbon bow to the handle.

Candy Cone

Secured by a trio of paper brads, this classy cone takes but minutes to create. Use the patterns on page 158 to cut the cone and decorative strip. Use glue stick to attach the strip to the background piece. Fold the edges together and punch the trio of holes through both layers. Secure layers together using prong-style brads.

Waving Flags

Swag a string of sporty paper flags as a colorful backdrop. Trace and enlarge the pattern on page 155. Use the pattern to cut triangles from decorative paper that coordinates with the color scheme. Using the pattern as a guide, punch four holes across the top of each flag. Thread the yarn in and out of the holes, then gently snug up each flag until it has a slight wave.

Bright Idea

Tones of pink, orange, and green come together in a very inviting color scheme. Mix prints and solids for a striking tabletop that sets a lively mood.

Doing the Derby

Invite friends over to cheer their favorite horses across the finish line. While these decorations lend themselves perfectly to televised horse races, the lively color scheme also can be used for occasions like bridal showers and birthday parties. An easy way to bring excitement to the table is to use scrapbook paper for place mats and fabric napkins as chair back covers.

Munch Buckets

Offer guests a sweet and salty snack in a pretty metal bucket. Poke gumdrops into candy gummy rings to appear as flowers amidst crisp white popcorn. Tie a ribbon bow to the handle, adding a rose trim to the center.

Sweet Sips

Transform beverage straws into decorative glass markers by taping on tiny paper pennants. Use the pattern on page 157 to cut each pennant from patterned paper and triangle from white. Use glue stick to attach the two pieces. Press on an adhesive rose embellishment and write "Win," "Place," or "Show" on each triangle. Wrap the pennant around the straw and tape in place.

Photo Favors

Capture race-day fun on film with photos of all party guests. If you have a photo printer, print copies before guests leave and insert them into frames to give to guests. To decorate each frame, cut a strip from patterned paper using the pattern on page 155. Fold over the strip and use a glue dot to hold in place. Trim with a mini rose and leaf.

Horsing Around

You'll want to hand-deliver these dimensional invitations. Adhere a narrow orange paper strip to the bottom of a pink paper rectangle. Mount the rectangle on a white notecard. Cut one wide and three narrow strips of paper to fit rectangle as shown. Use glue stick to hold the strips in place. Apply horse stickers and top with rose stickers. Seal the envelope with a rose embellishment.

Sunny Tablescapes

Make any meal a celebration with a table dressed in colors and blooms of the season.

Beautiful Calm

Celebrate the first patio party of the season. An easy flower-and-candle arrangement is a festive centerpiece—and the flickering flames are shielded from breezes. Fill a glass canister partway with sand then insert flower stems and candles. For longer-lasting blooms, use floral picks or moisten the sand.

Leafy Bouquets
A few roses in beds of lettuce put a budget-friendly spin on floral arrangements. Bright roses are showstopping against vivid green.

Border Plantings
A cloth in a springtime hue makes a gorgeous backdrop for the table arrangement. Attach scrapbooking daisies to create a dimensional border.

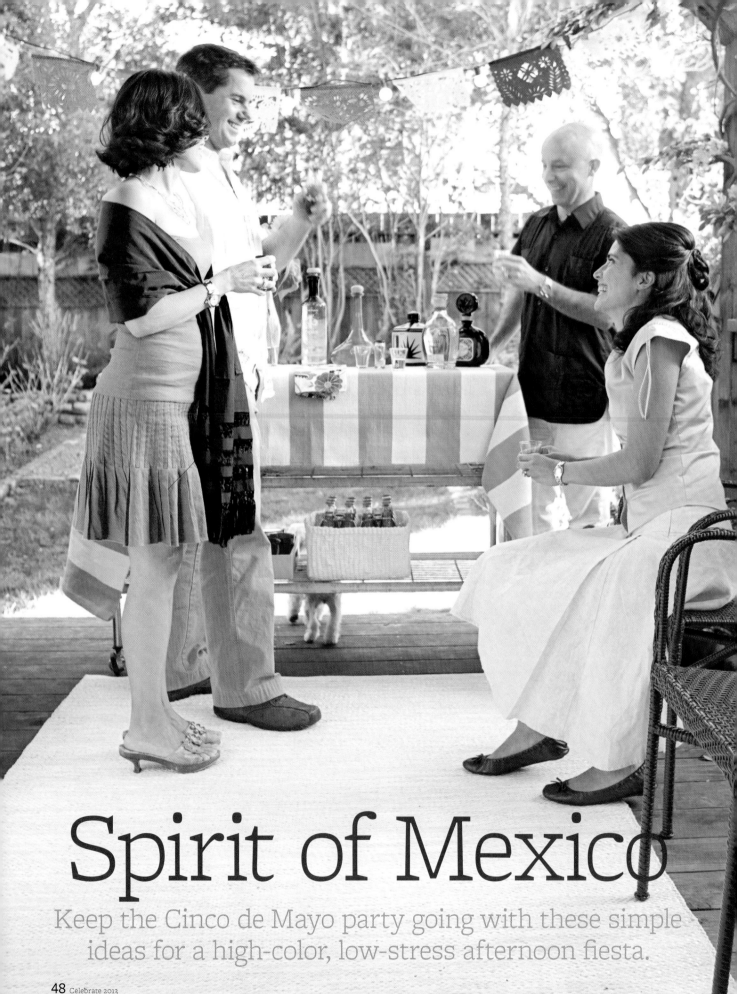

Spirit of Mexico

Keep the Cinco de Mayo party going with these simple ideas for a high-color, low-stress afternoon fiesta.

Initially Yours

Mark guests glasses with initial lime zesters. Skewer the lime slices and dangle one off each glass edge.

Bright Ideas

Sunflowers, propped in bottles for vases, add vibrancy to the table while tissue paper cutouts make a festive swag.

Take Homes

Wrap small potted cactus with bright tissue paper tied with ribbon. Poke in a sticker taped to a wood crafts stick.

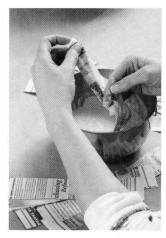

Maraca Piñata

Kids love candy, and this striped piñata is filled with more goodies than they can shake a stick at.

WHAT YOU'LL NEED
bowl; flour and water
newspaper, cut into strips
balloon
glue stick
crepe paper rolls in a variety of
  bright colors
wrapping paper tube, for handle
hot-glue gun and glue sticks

WHAT YOU DO
1. In a bowl, mix 2 cups flour with enough water to make a thick paste.
2. One by one, dip newspaper strips into the paste, pulling through fingers to remove excess as shown in Photo 1.
3. Cover the balloon surface with overlapping strips of paste-covered newspaper as shown in Photo 2. Add strips in this manner until the entire balloon has two layers. Let paste dry (this may take several days).
4. Cut a hole in the small end of the balloon using a crafts knife.
5. Apply glue stick around the opening. Begin covering with crepe paper, pleating as shown in Photo 3. Continue in this manner, changing colors to make stripes. For smooth stripes, simply wind the crepe paper around the balloon, holding in place with glue stick. Let dry.
6. Fill the piñata with candy.
7. Wrap the paper tube with crepe paper, holding in place with glue stick. Hot-glue the handle to the balloon as shown in Photo 4, covering the opening.
8. Tie long strands of crepe paper to the base of the handle.

Kiddie Bags

Invite kids to take home a surprise. Create paper-covered wood "bags" to match the bright color scheme. Trace the wood bag sides onto scrapbook paper, cut out, then adhere to wood using glue stick. Hot-glue chenille stems to define the edges. Tie a ribbon bow to one handle.

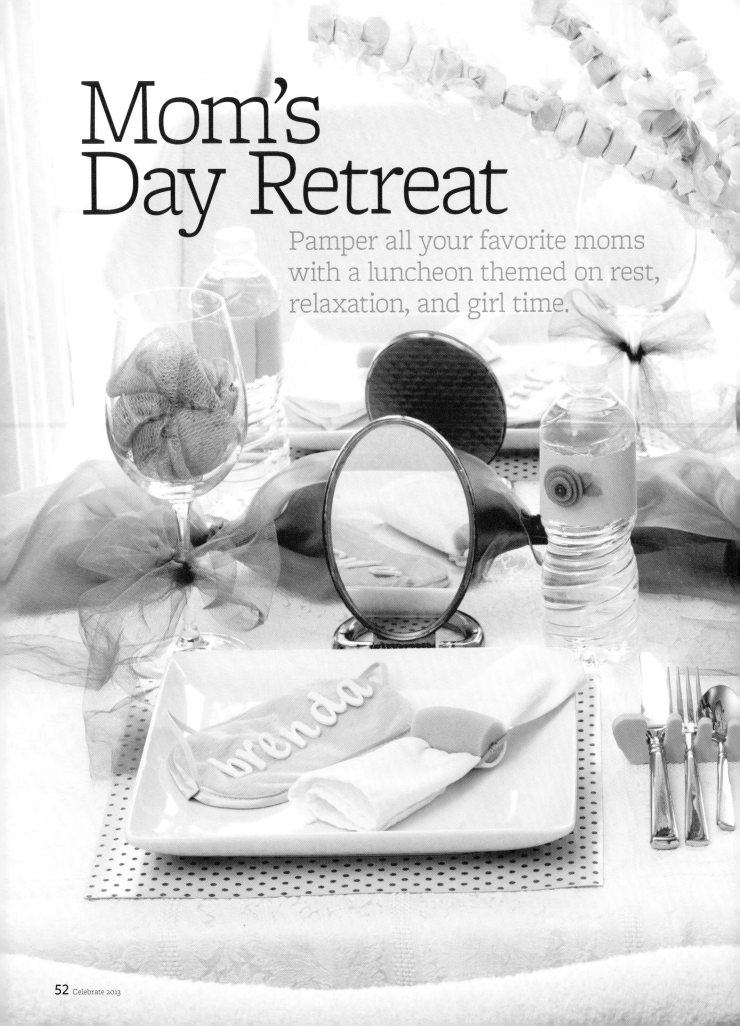

Mom's Day Retreat

Pamper all your favorite moms with a luncheon themed on rest, relaxation, and girl time.

Laugh and Taffy

Create an edible centerpiece by skewering wrapped pink and white saltwater taffy onto long wooden skewers. Simply string them onto the pointed end until the skewers are covered. Arrange stems in a pink glass vase.

Pretty in Pink

For feminine flair, pink in a range of tones sets the stage for an afternoon of girly gab. To enhance the spa-like atmosphere, cover a table with new oversize white terry cloth towels then ruffle tulle netting along the center.

Comfort Zone

In lieu of place cards, press foam stickers onto the backs of eye masks. Use a foam hair roller as a napkin ring and place a scrapbook paper place mat underneath the pampering arrangement.

Cozy Duo

Make a comfy no-sew chair cover using a large white bath towel. Pleat one end of the towel and secure with a pretty ribbon bow. Fold it over the chair top and pin in place with safety pins. Tuck in new cushy soft slippers for each guest.

Bottle Bloom

Hydrating has never been so fancy. Cut a paper strip using a decorative-edge scissor to wrap bottle. Using the patterns on page 158, cut out three felt circles as shown, stitch together with a button center and tack felt leaves to the back. Hot-glue the floral addition to the paper strip.

Silverware Stand

No pedicure needed for this clever usage of a nail painting assistant. Use brand-new cushioned holders to separate silverware instead of toes.

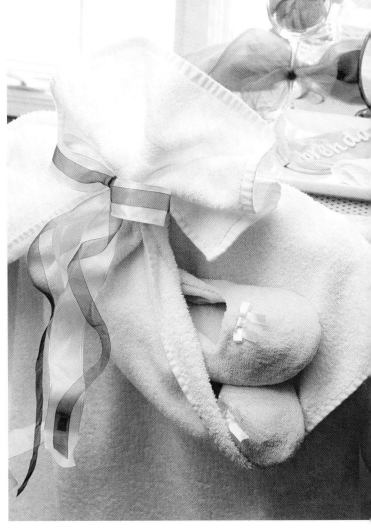

Ahoy, Graduate!

From life rings on the walls to starfish propped on the table and dangling over the edge, these nautical decorations are a swimming combination. The red, white, and navy, along with natural wood tones, add to the seaside attraction.

Seaside Graduation Gala

With most graduations taking place in the late spring, a seaside theme is fitting for the event and the season.

Natural Beauty

Crafts stores offer unfinished frames for painting. Leave them bare to blend in with the seascape. Driftwood pieces, scrubbed clean, add interesting shapes to the buffet table.

Stars and Stripes

Blanket the serving surface with layers of natural textures and tones to set off the navy blue embellishments.

Seashell Servers

Large shells are natural serving pieces to hold wrapped candies. Tuck in as many candies as the shells will hold and sprinkle more around them.

Guest Log

Create a clever guest book by covering a small journal with navy blue paper. Use adhesive metallic gold letters to write "passport" and the graduation year. Hot-glue seashells to natural jute and tie around the pen to use for signing.

Faith-Filled Gifts

Create works of vintage-style art that share a meaningful message for baptism, first communion, confirmation, or church membership day.

Picture of Faith

On an easel or hanging on the wall, this shabby chic picture shines with intriguing textures, layers, and handwritten details.

WHAT YOU'LL NEED
11×14-inch artist's canvas
acrylic paint in white and medium yellow
paintbrush
matte clear acrylic spray
10½×11-inch sheet of script-written scrapbook paper
decoupage medium
tracing paper
thick black marking pen
scissors; adhesive for fabric
13×1-inch strip of natural burlap
4×5-inch rectangle of natural burlap
penny
chipboard tag; rub-on black designs
hot-glue gun and glue sticks
5 decorative buttons
5 dimensional paper flower embellishments

WHAT YOU DO
1. Paint the canvas with white and medium yellow, blending the colors slightly to give the canvas an aged appearance; let dry.
2. Spray the canvas with clear acrylic spray; let dry.
3. Brush a coat of decoupage medium on the back of the scrapbook paper. Position on painted canvas, 1 inch from right edge. Press in place and let dry thoroughly.
4. Using the pattern on page 156 for placement, write the word "faith" in large letters on the scrapbook paper. Draw in the designs around the word as shown on pattern. For the large

scribbled circles, trace the pattern from page 157; cut out. Use circle to guide scribbles along lower edge as shown on placement guide.
5. Fray one long edge of the burlap strip. With fray on the left, glue the burlap strip to the left edge of the paper, wrapping burlap ends to the back of the canvas.
6. Fray the burlap rectangle, then glue on the strip, approximately 1½ inches from the bottom and ¾ inch from the left edge.

7. To make the scallop design along the right edge of the canvas, place a penny overlapping the paper edge and scribble around the edge of the penny. Draw dots along edge between scallops. Draw a leaf in the upper right corner of burlap rectangle.
8. Use rub-on designs to dot the "I" in lettering and to embellish chipboard tag. Draw on tag to include the style of the designs on the paper and canvas.
9. Hot-glue the buttons, flowers, and tag in place.

Bible Bookmark

Cut a 3×12-inch strip of natural burlap and fray the edges. Cut a 1½×10½-inch strip of script-written scrapbook paper. Using the pattern on page 157 as a guide, draw the motifs on the paper strip using a thick black marking pen. Scribble back and forth around a penny to make circular designs. Glue the paper strip onto burlap using adhesive for fabric and paper. Hot-glue a pair of dimensional paper flower embellishments to one edge.

Easy Does It
egg accents

Initially Marked

Paint wooden eggs. When dry, dip a pencil eraser into white paint and dot onto the surface. Hot-glue an initial charm onto each egg along with a small ribbon bow.

▲ Speckled Holder

A flat-bottom wooden egg makes the perfect place card holder for Easter dinner. If the egg doesn't stand upright, sand the bottom flat until it does. Use a fine saw to cut a slit in the top of the egg. Paint the egg using light blue acrylic paint; let dry. Dip an old toothbrush into white acrylic paint, run your thumb across it to splatter-paint the egg; let dry. Spray the painted egg with a clear top coat.

Pretty ▶ Bloomer

Whether you've dyed a blown-out egg or painted a wooden one, Easter eggs get dressed up in a jiffy using dimensional floral stickers. Choose a sticker to fit the egg and press in place. If desired, display in an egg cup.

Decoupaged Plant Pokes

Pastel-print napkins transform papier-mâché eggs into Easter beauties. If possible, separate napkin layers, using only the patterned layer. Cut a square large enough to cover the egg. Coat the egg with decoupage medium then gently press the napkin onto the egg. Brush a second coat of decoupage medium on the napkin; let dry. Poke the pointed end of a skewer into each egg; hot-glue in place. Tie a ribbon bow at base of egg, leaving long tails.

All Lined Up

Wrap eggs tightly with rubber bands then plunge into dye baths. Let the eggs dry before removing the rubber bands to reveal white stripes. For a similar look, draw on eggs with white crayon before dyeing.

Sparkle and Shine

Color real or artificial eggs using dye or paint. When dry, apply a coat of decoupage medium with a paintbrush. While wet, sprinkle the egg with matching glitter. Let the egg dry.

food

Showcase the most spectacular dishes at backyard barbecues, holiday dinners, game-day parties, and more. Beat summer heat with fabulously flavored lemonades.

Sweets for the Sweetheart

After treating your Valentine to a special candlelight dinner, what could be more romantic than indulging in decadent dessert?

MERINGUE-TOPPED
RASPBERRY CUPCAKES

Meringue-Topped Raspberry Cupcakes

Raspberry liqueur adds light, fruity flavor to these special cakes, crowned with crisp meringue topping.

PREP 25 minutes BAKE 23 minutes
COOL 5 minutes OVEN 350°F

1½ cups all-purpose flour
1½ teaspoons baking powder
¼   teaspoon salt
½   cup butter, softened
¾   cup sugar
1   egg
2   egg yolks
3   tablespoons raspberry liqueur or
    raspberry juice blend
1½ teaspoons vanilla
½   cup milk
4   egg whites
¼   teaspoon cream of tartar
⅔   cup sugar
12 raspberries (optional)

1. Preheat oven to 350°F. Line twelve 2½-inch muffin cups with paper bake cups or lightly coat muffin cups with nonstick spray for baking; set pan aside.
2. In a small bowl stir together flour, baking powder, and salt; set aside. In a large mixing bowl beat butter with an electric mixer on medium to high for 30 seconds. Add the ¾ cup sugar. Beat on medium to high for 1 minute, scraping sides of bowl occasionally. Beat in egg, egg yolks, raspberry liqueur, and vanilla until combined. Alternately add flour mixture and milk to butter mixture, beating on low after each addition just until combined.
3. Spoon batter into the prepared muffin cups, filling each about three-fourths full. Bake for 15 minutes.
4. Meanwhile, wash beaters thoroughly. In a medium mixing bowl combine egg whites and cream of tartar. Beat on medium until soft peaks form (tips curl). Gradually add the ⅔ cup sugar, 1 tablespoon at a time, beating on high until stiff peaks form (tips stand straight).
5. Pipe or spoon meringue on partially baked cupcakes. If desired, place a raspberry on each cupcake, pressing into meringue. Bake for 8 to 10 minutes more or until meringue is light brown.
6. Cool cupcakes in pan on a wire rack for 5 minutes. Remove cupcakes from pan; serve warm. (Or cover cupcakes loosely and chill up to 4 hours before serving.) Makes 12 cupcakes.

SIX-LAYER STRAWBERRY CAKE

Six-Layer Strawberry Cake

Treat your valentine to a towering layer cake filled with a luscious strawberry-and-lemon cream cheese frosting. Sliced fresh strawberries are a simply elegant topper.

PREP 1 hour BAKE 20 minutes
COOL 15 minutes CHILL 1½ hours
OVEN 350°F

    Nonstick cooking spray
3½ cups cake flour
1½ teaspoons baking soda
½   teaspoon salt
1   cup shortening
2   cups granulated sugar
2   tablespoons strawberry liqueur
2   teaspoons vanilla
    Red food coloring
1   cup buttermilk
1   cup finely chopped fresh strawberries
6   egg whites
1   teaspoon cream of tartar
2   8-ounce packages cream cheese,
    softened
1   cup butter, softened
¼   cup milk
2   teaspoons vanilla
1   teaspoon lemon extract
4   pounds powdered sugar
    Fresh strawberries

VANILLA DESSERT
SANDWICHES

1. Preheat oven to 350°F. Coat three 8×2-inch round cake pans with cooking spray. Line bottoms with waxed paper; coat waxed paper with cooking spray. Set pans aside. In a large bowl stir together flour, baking soda, and salt; set aside.

2. In an extra-large mixing bowl beat shortening with electric mixer on medium to high for 30 seconds. Gradually add 1½ cups granulated sugar, beating about 2 minutes or until well combined. Beat in liqueur, 2 teaspoons vanilla, and 10 drops food coloring. Alternately add flour mixture and buttermilk to sugar mixture, beating on low after each addition just until combined. Fold in ⅔ cup chopped strawberries.

3. Thoroughly wash beaters. In a large bowl combine egg whites and cream of tartar. Beat on medium until soft peaks form (tips curl). Gradually add remaining ½ cup granulated sugar, beating on high until stiff peaks form (tips stand straight). Fold about one-fourth of the beaten egg whites into cake batter to lighten. Fold in remaining beaten egg whites. Pour batter into prepared pans, spreading evenly.

4. Bake for 20 to 25 minutes or until tops spring back when lightly touched. Cool in pans on wire racks for 15 minutes. Remove from pans; remove waxed paper. Cool completely on racks.

5. For white frosting, in an extra-large mixing bowl combine 1 package of the cream cheese and ½ cup of the butter. Beat with an electric mixer on medium until smooth. Beat in 2 tablespoons of the milk, 1 teaspoon vanilla, and ½ teaspoon of the lemon extract. Gradually add 2 pounds of the powdered sugar, beating well.

6. For pink frosting, in another extra-large mixing bowl repeat Step 5 using remaining cream cheese, butter, milk, vanilla, lemon extract, and powdered sugar, except add 8 drops food coloring with the milk. Fold in remaining ⅓ cup chopped strawberries.

7. To assemble, use a long serrated knife to cut cake layers in half horizontally. Place one cake layer, cut side up, on a serving plate. Spread with 1 cup of the pink frosting. Place another cake layer, cut side down, on top of frosting. Spread with another 1 cup of the pink frosting. Repeat with three more cake layers and the remaining pink frosting. Top with the final cake layer, cut side down. Insert three or four long wooden skewers vertically into cake so layers do not slide. Loosely wrap with plastic wrap and chill for 30 minutes.

8. Frost sides of cake with about 3 cups of the white frosting. Remove skewers. Frost top of cake with the remaining white frosting. If desired, slice additional strawberries and arrange on top of cake.

TINY VANILLA CRÈME BRÛLÉES

Chill for 1 hour before serving. While cold, cut into wedges. Makes 10 servings.*

*Test Kitchen Tip: To easily cut cake, cut 10 wedges, then cut each wedge in half to make two 6-layer pieces. Or, place a small saucepan lid in center of the top of the cake. Using a long knife, cut around lid; remove lid. Cut outer circle of cake into 10 wedges, then cut inner circle into 10 wedges.

Vanilla Dessert Sandwiches

Make these light and delicate cookies and the frosting ahead of time then assemble just before serving.

PREP 45 minutes   CHILL 30 minutes
BAKE 10 minutes per batch   OVEN 350°F

3   cups unbleached all-purpose flour
2   teaspoons cream of tartar
1   teaspoon baking soda
½   teaspoon salt
1   cup unsalted butter, softened
1½   cups granulated sugar
2   tablespoons milk
1   tablespoon vanilla
2   teaspoons vanilla
1   recipe Vanilla Sugar
1   recipe Vanilla Cream Cheese Frosting

1. In a medium bowl whisk together flour, cream of tartar, baking soda, and salt. Set aside.

2. In a large mixing bowl beat butter with an electric mixer on medium for 30 seconds. Add granulated sugar and beat until smooth and creamy. Beat in milk, 1 tablespoon vanilla, and 2 teaspoons vanilla. Beat in as much of the flour mixture as you can with the mixer. Stir in remaining flour mixture by hand. Dough will be soft.

3. Divide dough in half. Cover and chill dough portions for about 30 minutes or until easy to handle. On lightly floured surface, roll half the dough at a time to ⅛-inch thickness.

4. Preheat oven to 350°F. Using a 3-inch scallop-edge round cutter, cut circles from dough. Using a 1-inch heart-shape cutter, cut centers of half the 3-inch circles. Place circles on parchment paper-lined cookie sheets. Reroll scraps, including the 1-inch

cutouts, and cut out additional circles as directed. Repeat with remaining dough half.

5. Sprinkle cookies with Vanilla Sugar. Bake cookies for 10 to 12 minutes or until golden brown. Cool on cookie sheets for 1 minute. Transfer to wire racks to cool completely.

6. Spread bottoms of the solid cookies with about 1½ teaspoons of the Vanilla Cream Cheese Frosting. Top with cookies with cutouts, sugar sides up. To store, refrigerate filled cookies. Makes 24 sandwich cookies.

Vanilla Sugar: Pour 4 cups sugar into a clean jar. Using a sharp paring knife, slit 1 vanilla bean lengthwise. Insert both halves into sugar, covering all of the bean with sugar. Secure lid and store in a cool, dry place for 2 weeks before using. (Will keep indefinitely.)

Vanilla Cream Cheese Frosting: In a medium bowl stir together 6 ounces cream cheese, softened; ¼ cup powdered sugar; and 1 teaspoon vanilla until smooth.

Tiny Vanilla Crème Brûlées

Anyone with a burning passion for this little French number will adore the mini versions.

PREP 35 minutes   STAND 15 minutes
BAKE 25 minutes   CHILL 4 hours
OVEN 300°F

1¾   cups whipping cream
½   cup sugar
¼   cup half-and-half or light cream
½   vanilla bean, split lengthwise
6   egg yolks
¼   cup sugar

1. Preheat oven to 300°F. In a heavy medium-size saucepan combine whipping cream, ½ cup sugar, and half-and-half. Using the tip of a small sharp knife, scrape out seeds from vanilla bean. Add vanilla seeds and pod to cream mixture. Cook and stir over medium heat just until mixture is boiling. Remove from heat. Cover and let stand for 15 minutes to infuse cream mixture with vanilla flavor. Remove vanilla pod; discard or reserve for another use.

2. Meanwhile, in a medium bowl whisk egg yolks until combined. Gradually whisk warm cream mixture into egg yolks.

3. Place ten 2-ounce ramekins in a 13×9×2-inch baking pan. Divide cream mixture evenly among ramekins. Place baking pan on an oven rack. Pour hot water into baking pan around ramekins to a depth of ¾ inch.

4. Bake for 25 to 30 minutes or until centers appear set when gently shaken. Carefully

remove ramekins from water; cool on a wire rack for 30 minutes. Cover and chill at least 4 hours.

5. To serve, sprinkle the ¼ cup sugar evenly on custards. Using a culinary blow torch, heat sugar until a bubbly brown crust forms.* Makes 10 servings.

***Test Kitchen Tip:** If ramekins are broiler-safe, melt the sugar under the broiler. Preheat the broiler. Return the chilled custards to the roasting pan and surround with ice cubes and a little cold water. Broil about 5 inches from the heat about 2 minutes or until a bubbly brown crust forms.

Strawberry Granita

Granitas—intensely fruit-flavored ices—are popular throughout Southern Italy. They're zippy, light, and refreshing. Serve them topped with Lemon Cream to make them even more decadent.

PREP **20 minutes** FREEZE **6 hours**

1⅓ cups water
⅔ cup sugar
4 cups fresh strawberries
1 tablespoon lemon juice
1 recipe Lemon Cream (optional)

1. For syrup, in a medium saucepan combine the water and sugar. Cook and stir over medium heat until sugar is dissolved; cool.

2. Place strawberries in a blender or food processor. Cover and blend or process until smooth (if necessary, add about ⅓ cup of the syrup to help puree the berries). Strain pureed strawberries through a fine-mesh sieve into a bowl; discard seeds. Stir strained pureed strawberries and lemon juice into syrup.

3. Pour mixture into a 2-quart square baking dish. Cover and freeze about 6 hours or until firm, stirring after 2 hours then after every hour.

4. Before serving, beat frozen mixture with a fork until fluffy. If desired, serve granita topped with Lemon Cream. Makes 8 to 10 servings.

Lemon Cream: In a small mixing bowl combine ⅓ cup whipping cream, 2 teaspoons sugar, and 1 teaspoon finely shredded lemon peel. Beat with an electric mixer on medium or with a wire whisk until soft peaks form (tips curl).

Triple-Berry Granita: Prepare as directed, except use 1½ cups fresh strawberries, 1½ cups fresh raspberries, and 1 cup fresh blueberries instead of just strawberries.

RASPBERRY PIE WITH CHAMBORD

Raspberry Pie with Chambord

PREP **40 minutes** BAKE **55 minutes** OVEN **375°F**

1 recipe Pastry for Single-Crust Pie
¾ cup granulated sugar
3 tablespoons cornstarch
5 cups fresh raspberries
¼ cup Chambord (black raspberry liqueur)
1 3-ounce package cream cheese, softened
⅓ cup powdered sugar
½ teaspoon vanilla
 Dash salt
¾ cup whipping cream
 Fresh red raspberries (optional)

1. Preheat oven to 375°F. Prepare Pastry for Single-Crust Pie. On a lightly floured surface, slightly flatten dough. Roll dough to a 12-inch circle. Transfer pastry to a 9-inch pie plate. Ease pastry into pie plate. Trim pastry 1 inch beyond edge of pie plate. Fold under extra pastry. Crimp edge as desired. Do not prick pastry.

2. For filling, in a large bowl combine granulated sugar and cornstarch. Add the raspberries and Chambord; toss gently to coat. Transfer filling to crust.

3. Cover edge of pie with foil to prevent overbrowning. Bake for 30 minutes. Remove foil. Bake for 25 to 30 minutes more or until filling is bubbly almost to the center and pastry is golden brown. Cool on a wire rack.

4. Before serving, in a medium mixing bowl beat cream cheese until smooth. Beat in powdered sugar, vanilla, and salt. In a large mixing bowl beat whipping cream until soft peaks form. Fold ⅓ cup of the whipped cream into cream cheese mixture. Fold in remaining whipped cream. Spread topping on pie. If desired, sprinkle with additional berries. Makes 8 servings.

Pastry for Single-Crust Pie: In a medium bowl stir together 1¼ cups all-purpose flour and ¼ teaspoon salt. Using a pastry blender, cut in ⅓ cup shortening until pieces are pea size. Sprinkle 1 tablespoon cold water over part of flour mixture; toss gently with a fork. Push to side of bowl. Repeat with additional cold water, 1 tablespoon at a time (4 to 5 tablespoons total), until all is moistened. Shape into a ball.

GLAZED EASTER HAM

Spring Fling

Create an Easter dinner as bright as the season.

Glazed Easter Ham

Tasty glaze and robust flavor make this perennial spring favorite welcome at the dinner table.

PREP **15 minutes** ROAST **2¼ hours** OVEN **325°F**

1 8- to 10-pound cooked boneless ham
1 recipe Lemon-Mustard, Stout, Apricot-Cherry, or Peach-Pineapple Glaze
1 recipe Mint and Lemon Sprinkle (optional)

1. Preheat oven to 325°F. Place ham on rack in roasting pan. Insert an oven-going meat thermometer into center. Bake, uncovered, for 2¼ to 2¾ hours* or until thermometer registers 140°F. Brush ham with desired glaze during the last 30 minutes of baking. If desired, serve with Mint and Lemon Sprinkle. Makes 16 to 20 (3-ounce) servings plus leftovers.

Lemon-Mustard Glaze: In a small bowl stir together ½ cup lemon curd; ¼ cup Dijon mustard; and 4 cloves garlic, minced. Makes ¾ cup glaze.

Stout Glaze: In a small saucepan combine ½ cup Irish stout or apple cider and ¼ cup *each* honey and butter. Bring to boiling; reduce heat. Simmer, uncovered, for 10 minutes. Makes ¾ cup glaze.

Apricot-Cherry Glaze: In a small bowl stir together ½ cup *each* apricot preserves and cherry preserves plus 1 tablespoon lemon juice. Makes 1 cup glaze.

Peach-Pineapple Glaze: In a saucepan combine one 8-ounce can crushed pineapple, undrained; ½ cup peach preserves; 2 tablespoons cider vinegar; and ½ teaspoon ground ginger. Stir until heated through. Makes 1¼ cups glaze.

Mint and Lemon Sprinkle: In a small bowl combine ½ cup snipped fresh mint; 1 tablespoon shredded lemon peel; and 2 cloves garlic, minced.

***Test Kitchen Tip:** If the ham weighs more than 8 pounds, cover it loosely with foil during the first 1 hour of roasting to prevent it from drying out.

Green Beans with Peppers and Pineapple

PREP **20 minutes** COOK **12 minutes**

2 pounds thin green beans
4 to 8 cloves garlic, thinly sliced
½ teaspoon crushed red pepper
2 tablespoons olive oil
1 small red sweet pepper, cut into thin strips
1 teaspoon finely shredded lime peel
2 tablespoons lime juice
½ fresh pineapple, peeled, cored, and cut into 6 or 7 slices

1. Wash beans and remove ends and strings. In a large Dutch oven bring lightly salted water to boiling. Add beans. Return to boiling; reduce heat. Simmer, covered, for 6 minutes or until beans are crisp-tender. Using a colander, drain and rinse beans under cold running water to stop cooking; drain again.

2. In a 12-inch skillet (with ventilation fan on) cook half the garlic and half the crushed red pepper in 1 tablespoon hot olive oil over medium-high heat for 15 seconds. Add half the green beans and cook, stirring frequently, for 2 to 3 minutes or until heated through. Season beans with *salt.* Remove from skillet. Repeat with remaining garlic, crushed red pepper, olive oil, and beans. Place all beans in a large serving dish.

3. Add pepper strips to the hot skillet and cook for 2 to 3 minutes. Toss beans with lime peel and juice. Top with pepper strips.

4. Add pineapple slices to the hot skillet. Cook for 4 minutes, turning once. Add pineapple to beans and peppers. Makes 12 side-dish servings.

GREEN BEANS WITH PEPPERS AND PINEAPPLE

CHEESY MASHED
POTATOES WITH
GOUDA AND CRISPY
PANCETTA

Cheesy Mashed Potatoes with Gouda and Crispy Pancetta

Pancetta is Italian cured pork belly that becomes very crispy with cooking, which adds pleasing texture to the creamy, cheesy potatoes.

START TO FINISH **40 minutes**

- 1 pound red-skin potatoes, cut into 1½-inch pieces
- 1 pound russet potatoes, peeled and cut into 1½-inch pieces
- 2 green onions
- 1 cup ¼-inch cubes pancetta (about 5 ounces)
- ¾ cup half-and-half, light cream, or whipping cream
- 2 cups finely shredded Gouda cheese (8 ounces)
  Salt
  Freshly ground black pepper

1. In a Dutch oven cook potatoes, covered, in enough boiling lightly salted water to cover for 20 to 25 minutes or until tender; drain. Return potatoes to Dutch oven.
2. Meanwhile, thinly slice green onions, separating white portions from green tops. Set green tops aside. In a medium skillet cook white portions of onions and pancetta over medium-high heat about 8 minutes or until pancetta is crisp, stirring occasionally. Drain off fat.
3. Add half-and-half to the cooked potatoes. Mash with potato masher or beat mixture with an electric mixer on low until nearly smooth. Add 1½ cups of the cheese and the pancetta mixture. Season to taste with salt and pepper.
4. Transfer mashed potatoes to a serving dish. Sprinkle with green onion tops and the remaining ½ cup cheese. Makes 8 to 10 side-dish servings.

Crisp Cornmeal Scones

These nibble-size scones are easy to mix. Instead of cutting in the butter, just shred it on a grater and toss it in.

PREP **15 minutes** BAKE **12 minutes** OVEN **425°F**

- 2 cups all-purpose flour
- 1 cup yellow cornmeal
- 2 tablespoons granulated sugar
- 1½ teaspoons baking powder
- ½ teaspoon salt
- ½ cup cold butter, coarsely shredded or cubed*
  1 cup buttermilk
  Buttermilk
  Coarse sugar

CRISP CORNMEAL SCONES
SWEET TOMATO JAM

1. Preheat oven to 425°F. In a large bowl whisk together flour, cornmeal, granulated sugar, baking powder, and salt.
2. Add shredded butter to flour mixture; toss to distribute. (Or cut cubed butter into flour mixture with pastry blender until it resembles coarse crumbs.)
3. Make a well in the center of the flour and butter mixture. Add 1 cup buttermilk; stir with a spoon just until moistened. Do not overmix. (If dough appears dry, add 1 to 2 tablespoons additional buttermilk.)
4. Turn dough out onto a floured surface. Gently knead by lifting and folding dough, 4 or 5 times, giving a quarter turn after each knead. Roll into 8-inch square, ¾ inch thick. Cut into 1½- to 2-inch squares.
5. Place squares 1 inch apart on an ungreased baking sheet. Brush with buttermilk; sprinkle with coarse sugar. Bake for 12 to 15 minutes or until lightly browned. Cool scones on a wire rack. Serve warm. Makes 16 to 25 scones.
*Test Kitchen Tip: To easily shred butter, first freeze it for 15 minutes. Using a grater, coarsely shred the cold butter. Toss it into the flour mixture or refrigerate the shreds, loosely covered, until needed.

Sweet Tomato Jam

Sharp tomatoes, cooked down with sugar, and a hint of spices, soften to a sweetly spreadable jam.

PREP **10 minutes** COOK **35 minutes** COOL **1 hour**

- 1 pound plum tomatoes, coarsely chopped (3 cups)
- ½ pound red and/or yellow cherry or grape tomatoes, halved (1¾ cups)
- ½ cup sugar
- ½ teaspoon ground cinnamon
- ¼ teaspoon crushed red pepper (optional)

1. In saucepan combine tomatoes, sugar, cinnamon, and crushed red pepper. Bring to boiling, stirring often. Reduce heat; cook, uncovered, over medium-low heat for 35 minutes or until thickened, stirring occasionally. Remove from heat. Transfer to a bowl and cool.
2. Serve immediately or cover and refrigerate up to 3 days. Makes 8 (¼-cup) servings.

CLASSIC COCONUT CAKE
WITH FROSTING

Classic Coconut Cake with Frosting

This scrumptious three-layer cake is enveloped in fluffy frosting and coconut. Let it be the grand finale for an Easter brunch or dinner.

PREP 1¼ hours   BAKE 20 minutes
OVEN 350°F

5   eggs
1   cup unsalted butter
1   cup whole milk
3   cups sifted cake flour
1   tablespoon baking powder
½   teaspoon kosher salt
2   cups sugar
1   tablespoon vanilla
1   fresh coconut, husk and peel removed
    and grated or finely shredded (3 to
    4 cups)
3   egg whites
2   cups sugar
¼   teaspoon cream of tartar
¾   cup water
¼   teaspoon kosher salt
2   teaspoons pure vanilla extract

1. Let eggs, butter, and milk stand at room temperature for 30 minutes. Preheat oven to 350°F. In a medium bowl combine cake flour, baking powder, and kosher salt; spoon flour mixture onto a square of waxed paper. Butter three 8×8×2-inch square or three 8×1½-inch round cake pans; line bottoms with waxed paper. Butter waxed paper and lightly flour; set aside.
2. In large mixing bowl beat butter with an electric mixer on medium to high for 30 seconds. Add the 2 cups sugar and 1 tablespoon vanilla; beat for 3 to 4 minutes on medium until well combined. Add eggs, one at a time, beating well after each addition. Using waxed paper as a funnel, alternately add flour mixture and milk to butter mixture, beating on low after each addition just until combined. Divide batter among the three pans.
3. Bake for 20 to 25 minutes or until tops spring back when lightly touched. Cool in pans on wire racks for 10 minutes. Remove cakes from pans; peel off and discard waxed paper. Cool cakes on wire racks.
4. For coconut, with an ice pick or nut pick, make holes in two of the eyes with a pressing, twisting motion. If eyes are especially tough, tap top of pick with hammer. Pour coconut water into a large measuring cup. If desired, cover and save for another use.
5. To crack the coconut shell, hold the coconut in one hand and tap with hammer—somewhat assertively—rotating coconut as you strike. After 2 to 3 minutes

HERB SALAD WITH CREAMY LEMON DRESSING

listen for a change in tapping sound and then a cracking sound, which indicates the shell has split. Separate coconut into pieces, tapping with hammer as necessary.
6. Remove coconut meat to a towel-protected counter. Slowly work thin-bladed knife between coconut and shell. With a vegetable peeler, remove brown skin from coconut. Using the smallest holes on a box grater, shred coconut.
7. To make the sugar syrup, let egg whites stand at room temperature for 30 minutes. In a medium saucepan combine 2 cups sugar, cream of tartar, and water. Cook and stir over low heat until sugar is dissolved. Cover; bring to boiling. Boil for 2 minutes. Remove cover; attach a candy thermometer to pan and cook, without stirring, until thermometer reads 240°F (5 to 10 minutes).
8. Meanwhile, in large mixing bowl beat egg whites with an electric mixer on medium to high until frothy. Add ¼ teaspoon salt; beat just until stiff peaks begin to form.
9. With mixer on low, slowly pour in hot syrup. Beat in the 2 teaspoons vanilla. Increase speed to medium-high; beat until light and fluffy and a dollop of whites lifted off beater holds its shape (3 to 4 minutes).
10. To assemble cake, on a serving plate or stand arrange each cake layer and spread with frosting, then sprinkle generously with coconut. If frosting thickens, set over bowl of hot water. When the cake is completely frosted, heap with additional coconut,

pressing gently with fingers to bed the coconut. Makes 16 servings.

Herb Salad with Creamy Lemon Dressing

A simple and refreshing combo of butterhead lettuce and herbs tossed with a lemony sour cream dressing creates the perfect spring salad.

START TO FINISH 20 minutes

    Finely shredded peel and juice
    from 2 medium lemons
3   cloves garlic, minced
2   teaspoons Dijon mustard
½   cup olive oil
½   cup sour cream
2   to 3 medium heads butterhead
    lettuce, torn, or 6 to 8 cups mixed
    baby salad greens
1½ cups assorted fresh herbs, such as
    chives, basil, parsley, or mint, torn
12 to 16 radishes, thinly sliced

1. For dressing, combine lemon peel and juice, garlic, mustard, and ¼ teaspoon *each salt* and *pepper*. Slowly whisk in oil until thickened. Whisk in sour cream.
2. In a bowl toss together lettuce and herbs; transfer to a serving platter. Top with sliced radishes; pass dressing. Makes 6 to 8 side-dish servings.

Juicy, Sweet Watermelon

This succulent summertime refresher pleases the palate in so many ways— from small bites and grilled salads to lively soups and drinks.

Watermelon-Prosciutto Bites

Rich and tangy goat cheese (chèvre) creates a salty-sweet sensation when paired with summer's favorite fruit. With its fruity and refreshing flavor, the melon offers a deeply sweet contrast to the goat cheese's robust flavor.

START TO FINISH **30 minutes**

- 8 cups seedless watermelon chunks (3 pounds)
- 4 ounces goat cheese (chèvre), sliced
- 5 ounces thinly sliced prosciutto, cut into 1-inch strips
- 2 tablespoons olive oil
- 1 tablespoon lime juice or lemon juice
  Freshly ground black pepper (optional)
  Lime or lemon wedges (optional)

1. Thread each watermelon chunk onto a cocktail pick or toothpick; add a slice of cheese. Fold each prosciutto strip accordian-style; thread on pick.

2. Arrange picks on a large serving platter. In a small bowl combine oil and lime juice; drizzle over watermelon, cheese, and prosciutto. If desired, sprinkle with ground black pepper and serve with lime or lemon wedges. Makes 8 to 10 servings.

To Make Ahead: Assemble watermelon bites as directed, except do not drizzle with the oil mixture. Cover and chill for up to 6 hours. Before serving, drizzle the watermelon bites with the oil mixture and sprinkle with ground black pepper, if desired.

Watermelon Artistry

Impress guests with a beautiful watermelon centerpiece—the perfect way to serve fresh fruit salad at a party, picnic, or special gathering.

START TO FINISH **40 minutes**

1   large round seedless watermelon
    Sharp knife
    Sharp pencil or thin dry-erase marker
    Utility knife or carving knife
    Melon baller
    1-inch star-shape cookie cutter
1   medium cantaloupe
1   medium honeydew melon
6   to 8 long, narrow wooden skewers

1. Wash the watermelon and pat dry. Cut a ¼-inch slice off one end to provide a stable base. Using a sharp pencil or thin marker, draw a scallop design around the upper middle portion of the watermelon. Use a utility knife to carve the design.
2. Split watermelon open at scalloped edge. Use a melon baller to remove flesh from watermelon base. Slice remaining watermelon half into thick slices and cut out several stars. Cut melon balls and star shapes from the cantaloupe and honeydew melon. Fill watermelon base with melon pieces. Alternately thread melon stars and balls onto skewers. Insert skewers into the melon base.

Grilled Chicken with Watermelon Glaze

A chile-spiked watermelon glaze creates the heat—and the sweet—that makes this a finger-licking-good barbecued chicken. Use glaze immediately or store tightly covered in the refrigerator for up to 2 days.

PREP **40 minutes**   GRILL **50 minutes**
STAND **10 minutes**

1   small watermelon
1   12-ounce jar apple jelly
    Juice and zest of 1 small lime
2   teaspoons red chile flakes
1   teaspoon jalapeño hot sauce
1   whole chicken or 3½ pounds meaty chicken pieces
    Olive oil
    Snipped fresh herbs (optional)

1. For watermelon glaze, cut half of the watermelon from the rind in chunks (about 4 cups of fruit). Cut remaining half of watermelon into wedges for serving; refrigerate until ready to serve. Place in a food mill or juicer and collect the juice. Or place watermelon chunks in a blender. Cover; blend until nearly smooth. Pour mixture into a fine mesh sieve over a bowl; discard solid bits. Reserve 1 cup of the juice for glaze; drink or freeze the rest.
2. In a small saucepan melt jelly over low heat, stirring often so it doesn't burn. Stir in 1 cup watermelon juice, the lime juice, and zest. Add red chile flakes, jalapeño hot sauce, and a pinch of *salt*. Mix and taste. Adjust seasoning as desired and remove from heat. Reserve ⅓ cup of the glaze to pass at serving time.
3. To prepare chicken, remove chicken from packaging and pat dry with paper towels. To butterfly*, using poultry or kitchen shears cut along each side of backbone to remove it. Turn chicken breast-side up. Open the two sides of the chicken as if opening a book and lay them flat. Break breastbone by firmly applying pressure and pressing down. Tuck wing tips under upper wings.
4. Prepare grill for indirect grilling. Brush chicken with olive oil. Season on both sides with *salt* and *ground black pepper*. Place skin-side down, on center of grill over indirect medium heat.
5. Grill chicken for 25 minutes. Turn chicken over. Brush some of the remaining ⅔ cup glaze on skin. Grill chicken for 25 to 30 minutes more or until juices run clear and an instant-read thermometer inserted in thickest part of thigh registers 180°F, brushing with glaze twice more.
6. Remove chicken from grill. Let chicken rest for 10 minutes. Cut chicken into pieces. Serve with fresh watermelon wedges and sprinkle with herbs. Pass reserved ⅓ cup glaze to spoon over top. Makes 6 servings.

WATERMELON, MANGO, AND JICAMA SALSA

WATERMELON SOUP WITH FRESH MINT

*Test Kitchen Tip: Butterflying makes it easy to cook a whole chicken on the grill. Poultry or kitchen shears are the best tool for the job. Make a cut about 1½ inches apart on both sides of the backbone, cutting all the way down, and remove backbone.

Watermelon, Mango, and Jicama Salsa

This exotic salsa makes 24 servings for a simple and sassy side dish.

START TO FINISH **30 minutes**

3   cups chopped seeded watermelon
1½   cups chopped peeled jicama
1   cup chopped peeled mango
2   tablespoons chopped green onion (1)
1   medium fresh jalapeño chile pepper, seeded and finely chopped*
1   tablespoon snipped fresh cilantro
1   tablespoon lime juice
⅛   teaspoon cayenne pepper

1. In a medium bowl stir together watermelon, jicama, mango, green onion, jalapeño pepper, cilantro, lime juice, and cayenne pepper.
2. If desired, cover and chill for up to 24 hours. Serve with grilled pork, chicken, or fish. Makes 24 (¼-cup) servings.
*Test Kitchen Tip: Because chile peppers contain volatile oils that can burn your skin and eyes, avoid direct contact with them as much as possible. When working with chile peppers, wear plastic or rubber gloves. If

your bare hands touch the peppers, wash your hands and nails well with soap and warm water.

Watermelon Soup with Fresh Mint

Whether you throw a spring shindig or a patio pool party, pureed soup this refreshing begs to be on the menu as an appetizer or dessert.

PREP **20 minutes**   CHILL **2 hours**

4   cups diced seedless watermelon
2   tablespoons freshly squeezed lemon juice
2   tablespoons freshly squeezed lime juice
1   tablespoon chopped fresh mint
1   tablespoon honey
¼   teaspoon ground ginger
      Watermelon wedges

1. In a blender or food processor combine watermelon, lemon juice, lime juice, chopped mint, honey, and ginger. Cover and blend or process until nearly smooth. Cover and chill for 2 to 4 hours.
2. To serve, ladle soup into bowls. Top each serving with a watermelon wedge. Makes 4 servings.

Grilled Watermelon-Shrimp Salad

PREP 30 minutes **GRILL** 8 minutes

- 1 pound fresh or frozen large shrimp in shells
- 6 tablespoons olive oil
- ½ teaspoon kosher salt or salt
- ¼ cup lemon juice
- 2 tablespoons honey
- 1 teaspoon crushed red pepper
- 1 1½-inch slice seedless watermelon (2¼ to 2½ pounds), quartered
- 1 5- to 6-ounce package torn mixed salad greens
- ½ cup crumbled Gorgonzola cheese or other blue cheese (2 ounces)

1. Thaw shrimp, if frozen. Peel and devein shrimp, leaving tails intact (if desired). Rinse shrimp; pat dry with paper towels. Thread shrimp onto four 10- to 12-inch wooden or metal skewers,* leaving ¼ inch between pieces. Brush shrimp with 2 tablespoons of the oil and sprinkle with ¼ teaspoon of the salt.

2. In a small bowl whisk together the remaining 4 tablespoons oil, the remaining ¼ teaspoon salt, lemon juice, honey, and crushed red pepper. Brush watermelon with some of the lemon juice mixture.

3. For a charcoal grill, grill shrimp kabobs and watermelon on the rack of an uncovered grill directly over medium coals until shrimp are opaque and watermelon is warm and grill marks are visible, turning once halfway through grilling. Allow 4 to 6 minutes for shrimp and 8 to 10 minutes for watermelon. (For a gas grill, preheat grill. Reduce heat to medium. Place shrimp kabobs and watermelon on grill rack over heat. Cover and grill as above.)

4. To serve, divide salad greens among four dinner plates. Top with shrimp kabobs and watermelon. Whisk the remaining lemon juice mixture until combined; drizzle over salads. Sprinkle with cheese. Makes 4 servings.

*****Test Kitchen Tip:** If using wooden skewers, soak for at least 30 minutes in enough water to cover. Drain before using. If desired, use double wooden or metal skewers for more stability.

GRILLED WATERMELON-
SHRIMP SALAD

Stuffed Baby Watermelon

Watermelon will never taste better than in this lime- and honey-tossed medley of melon, peaches, and grapes.

START TO FINISH **30 minutes**

- 1   teaspoon finely shredded lime peel
- 2   tablespoons lime juice
- 1   tablespoon honey
- 1   8-inch baby watermelon (about 5 pounds) or 7 cups seedless watermelon balls or cubes
- ¾   cup sliced white or yellow peach or nectarine
- ½   cup seedless red grapes, halved Lime peel strips (optional)

1. In a large bowl combine finely shredded lime peel, lime juice, and honey; set aside.
2. If using baby watermelon, cut in half crosswise. Using a melon baller, scoop out flesh. Add watermelon balls or cubes to lime mixture. Add peach and grapes; toss gently to coat.
3. If desired, serve fruit in baby watermelon halves and garnish with lime peel strips. Makes 6 servings.

STUFFED BABY WATERMELON

WATERMELON-BASIL LEMONADE

Watermelon-Basil Lemonade

Turn this lovely lemonade into a lively libation by adding your favorite watermelon vodka, a favorite summertime upscale cocktail perfect for entertaining.

PREP **25 minutes** CHILL **2 hours**

- ¼   cup fresh basil leaves
- 4   cups boiling water
- 1   cup freshly squeezed lemon juice (reserve lemon rinds)
- ½   to ¾ cup sugar
- 3   cups pureed watermelon Watermelon wedges Lemon slices

1. In a 4-quart heat-proof bowl, bruise basil leaves with the back of a wooden spoon. Add boiling water, lemon juice, and sugar, stirring to dissolve sugar. Stir in pureed watermelon and the reserved lemon rinds. Cover and chill for 2 to 3 hours. Remove and discard rinds.
2. Strain lemonade through a fine-mesh sieve into a large pitcher. Garnish with fresh watermelon wedges and lemon slices. Stir before serving. Serve in ice-filled glasses. Makes 6 (10-ounce) servings.

Tailgate Party

Throw a fun and stylish football fete that will be a crowd-pleaser all around.

Ultimate Chili Dogs

PREP 20 minutes   BAKE 17 minutes
OVEN 400°F

8   4-ounce beef hot dogs
8   slices bacon
1   small white onion
8   extra-long hot dog buns or hoagie buns, split and toasted
1½ cups Bowl of Red (recipe, page 89)
4   slices American cheese, halved diagonally
⅓   cup seeded and finely chopped roma tomato (1 medium)
16 to 24 slices pickled jalapeño chile peppers
¼   cup crushed corn chips or tortilla chips (optional)

1. Preheat oven to 400°F. Line a 15×10×1-inch baking pan with foil. Wrap hot dogs with bacon; secure with wooden toothpicks, if necessary. Place hot dogs in prepared baking pan. Bake for 17 to 20 minutes or until bacon is crisp.
2. Finely chop onion and rinse in a colander to remove sharpness for a milder onion flavor; drain well.
3. Place hot dogs in buns. Top with Bowl of Red, cheese, onion, tomato, jalapeño slices, and, if desired, crushed corn chips. Makes 8 servings.

Twisted Buffalo Wings

It wouldn't be a tailgate without a batch of the ever-popular appetizer wings. These succulent, tasty morsels heat up nicely in a slow cooker and deliver a flavor kick like no other.

PREP 35 minutes   BROIL 15 minutes
CHILL overnight

16 chicken wings (about 3½ pounds total)
1   12-ounce bottle chili sauce
3   tablespoons bottled hot pepper sauce
2   tablespoons butter, softened
1   recipe Blue Cheese Dip
    Celery sticks

TWISTED BUFFALO WINGS

1. Preheat broiler. Cut off and discard tips of chicken wings. Cut wings at joints to form 32 pieces. Place chicken wing pieces on the unheated rack of a broiler pan. Broil 4 to 5 inches from the heat for 15 to 20 minutes or until tender and no longer pink, turning once; cool slightly. Place chicken pieces in a storage container.
2. Combine chili sauce, hot pepper sauce, and butter. Pour sauce mixture over chicken pieces; cover and chill overnight.
3. Transfer chicken mixture to a 3½- or 4-quart slow cooker that has a car adapter. Cover and heat on high-heat setting for 2 to 2½ hours or until heated through.
4. Tightly cover slow cooker and tote in an insulated carrier. Tote Blue Cheese Dip and celery in an insulated cooler with ice packs.

5. At the tailgating site, plug slow cooker into car adapter and keep chicken wings warm on warm-heat setting. Serve with Blue Cheese Dip and celery sticks. Provide moist towelettes when serving. Makes 16 servings.
Blue Cheese Dip: In a blender or food processor combine ½ cup sour cream, ½ cup mayonnaise, ½ cup crumbled blue cheese, 1 tablespoon white wine vinegar or white vinegar, and 1 clove garlic, minced. Cover and blend or process until smooth. Cover and chill for up to 1 week. If desired, top with additional crumbled blue cheese before serving. Makes 1¼ cups.

Fudgy Football Brownies

After indulging in a savory spread, these sweet treats are welcome and satisfying.

PREP 30 minutes BAKE 18 minutes
STAND overnight OVEN 350°F

1   cup butter
6   ounces unsweetened chocolate, coarsely chopped
2   cups sugar
4   eggs
2   teaspoons vanilla
1⅓ cups all-purpose flour
½   teaspoon baking soda
1   cup miniature semisweet chocolate pieces
      Creamy Vanilla Frosting or 1 cup canned vanilla frosting

1. In a medium saucepan combine butter and unsweetened chocolate. Cook and stir over low heat until melted; cool slightly. Preheat oven to 350°F. Line a 15×10×1-inch baking pan with foil, extending the foil over edges of pan. Grease foil; set pan aside.
2. Stir sugar into chocolate mixture. Add eggs, one at a time, beating with a wooden spoon after each addition just until combined. Stir in vanilla. In a small bowl stir together flour and baking soda. Add flour mixture to chocolate mixture, stirring just until combined. Stir in semisweet chocolate pieces. Pour batter into the prepared baking pan, spreading evenly.
3. Bake for 18 minutes. Cool in pan on a wire rack. Using the edges of the foil, lift brownies out of pan. Using a 3- to 4-inch football-shape or other cookie cutter, cut out brownies. (Or cut brownies into rectangles.)
4. Spoon Creamy Vanilla Frosting into a decorating bag fitted with a small round tip. Pipe frosting onto brownies to decorate. Let stand until frosting is set.
5. Layer brownies in a storage container between sheets of waxed paper. Cover container tightly and let stand at room temperature overnight.
6. Tote brownies in container at room temperature. Makes 9 or 10 football brownies or 48 brownie rectangles.
Serving suggestion: To use up the brownie scraps, coarsely crumble scraps. Layer about one-third of the scraps in a 1-quart canning jar. Pipe additional frosting on crumbles. Repeat layering twice. If desired, top the last layer of frosting with chocolate-flavored sprinkles. Seal jar and let stand at room temperature overnight. On tailgate day tote in jar at room temperature. Use a spoon to scoop servings onto plates.
Creamy Vanilla Frosting: In a large mixing bowl combine ¼ cup shortening and 1 teaspoon vanilla. Beat with an electric mixer on medium for 30 seconds. Gradually beat in ¾ cup powdered sugar. Beat in 2 teaspoons milk. Gradually beat in ¾ cup additional powdered sugar. If necessary, beat in additional milk, 1 teaspoon at a time, to make frosting of piping consistency.

FUDGY FOOTBALL BROWNIES

Slow Cooker Carnitas

Set out an array of toppings and let tailgaters customize this south-of-the-border sandwich to their tastes.

PREP 35 minutes SLOW-COOK 8 hours (low) or 4 hours (high)
CHILL overnight

1½ teaspoons garlic powder
1   teaspoon salt
1   teaspoon dried oregano, crushed
1   teaspoon ground coriander
1   teaspoon ground cumin
1   teaspoon ground ancho chile pepper or chili powder
¼   teaspoon ground cinnamon
1   5-pound boneless pork shoulder roast
2   tablespoons vegetable oil
2   bay leaves
1   cup chicken broth
2   teaspoons finely shredded lime peel
      Desired toppings (chopped tomato, slivered red onion, shredded cheddar cheese, guacamole, sour cream, salsa, and/or fresh cilantro leaves)
12 to 16 (8-inch) flour tortillas

1. In a large bowl combine garlic powder, salt, oregano, coriander, cumin, ground ancho pepper, and cinnamon; set aside. Trim fat from meat. Cut meat into 2-inch pieces. Add meat to spice mixture; toss gently to coat.
2. In a large skillet heat oil over medium-high heat. Cook meat, one-third at a time, in hot oil until brown. Using a slotted spoon, transfer meat to a 4½- or 5-quart slow cooker that has a car adapter. Add bay leaves. Pour broth over meat.
3. Cover and cook on low-heat setting for 8 to 10 hours or on high-heat setting for 4 to 5 hours. Using a slotted spoon, remove meat from cooker, reserving cooking liquid. Remove and discard bay leaves. Using two forks, pull meat apart into coarse shreds. Transfer shredded meat to a storage container; stir in the reserved cooking liquid and lime peel. Cover and chill meat mixture overnight.
4. Return meat and liquid to slow cooker. Cover and reheat on high-heat setting about 2 hours or until heated through.
5. Tightly cover slow cooker and tote in an insulated carrier. Tote desired toppings in an insulated cooler with ice packs.
6. At the tailgating site, plug slow cooker into car adapter and keep meat mixture warm on warm-heat setting. To serve, spoon meat mixture onto tortillas; add toppings. Fold each tortilla over filling. Fold in sides; roll up tortilla. Makes 12 to 16 servings.

Bowl of Red

Texans have a high tolerance for hot and spicy foods, so if you're not from the Lone Star State, taste the authentic, extra-hot chili at your own risk!

PREP 20 minutes COOK 40 minutes

1½ pounds ground beef chuck
1 cup chopped onion (1 large)
3 cloves garlic, minced
1 tablespoon ground pasilla or ancho chile pepper
1 teaspoon salt
1 teaspoon ground cumin
1 teaspoon paprika
1 teaspoon dried oregano, crushed
¼ teaspoon cayenne pepper
⅛ teaspoon ground cloves
1 14.5-ounce can diced tomatoes, undrained
1 14.5-ounce can beef broth
1 12-ounce bottle lager beer or 1½ cups beef broth
1 tablespoon yellow mustard
1 8-ounce carton sour cream
1 tablespoon snipped fresh cilantro
   Finely chopped red onion

1. In a Dutch oven cook ground beef, the 1 cup onion, and garlic over medium-high heat until meat is brown, using a wooden spoon to break up meat as it cooks. Drain off fat. Stir in pasilla pepper, salt, cumin, paprika, oregano, cayenne pepper, and cloves. Cook and stir for 2 to 3 minutes or until fragrant.
2. Stir in tomatoes, broth, beer, and mustard. Bring to boiling; reduce heat. Simmer, uncovered, about 40 minutes or until desired consistency.
3. In a small bowl combine sour cream and cilantro. Top each serving of chili with sour cream mixture and red onion. Makes 6 servings.

Slow Cooker Directions: Prepare as directed in Step 1. Transfer meat mixture to a 3½- or 4-quart slow cooker. Stir in tomatoes, broth, ½ cup of the beer (reserve remaining beer for another use), and the mustard. Cover and cook on low-heat setting for 8 to 10 hours or on high-heat setting for 5 hours. Serve as directed.

Bloody Mary Beer

Horseradish adds a nice bite to this refreshing drink. Try other garnishes, such as beef jerky, cooked shrimp, and pickles.

PREP 15 minutes CHILL overnight

4 cups vegetable juice
2 tablespoons lemon juice
2 tablespoons prepared horseradish

BLOODY MARY BEER

4 teaspoons Worcestershire sauce
2 teaspoons celery seeds
¼ teaspoon ground black pepper
   Ice cubes
4 12- to 16-ounce bottles beer or nonalcoholic beer
   Celery sticks, pitted olives, and/or lime wedges (optional)
   Bottled hot pepper sauce

1. In a 3-quart insulated jug combine vegetable juice, lemon juice, horseradish, Worcestershire sauce, celery seeds, and pepper. Cover and chill overnight.
2. Tote vegetable juice mixture in the chilled jug. Tote ice cubes, beer, and, if desired, celery, olives, and/or lime wedges in an insulated cooler.
3. At the tailgating site, for each drink, half-fill a 12-ounce glass with ice cubes. Pour in one-half bottle of beer. Fill glass with vegetable juice mixture; add hot pepper sauce to taste. Garnish drinks with celery, olives, and/or lime wedges. Makes 8 (10-ounce) servings.

Greek Pasta Salad

The fresh herbs, oils, and olives that characterize Greek cuisine complement the mostaccioli in this sprightly pasta salad. A flourish of feta cheese on top adds a sharp, salty bite.

PREP 35 minutes CHILL overnight

12 ounces dried mostaccioli or penne pasta
2 cups cherry tomatoes, quartered
1 medium cucumber, halved lengthwise and sliced
½ cup sliced green onions (4)
⅓ cup pitted Kalamata olives, halved
½ cup vegetable oil
½ cup lemon juice
2 tablespoons snipped fresh basil or 2 teaspoons dried basil, crushed

2 tablespoons snipped fresh oregano or 2 teaspoons dried oregano, crushed
4 to 6 cloves garlic, minced
¼ teaspoon salt
¼ teaspoon ground black pepper
1 cup crumbled feta cheese (4 ounces)
   Fresh oregano leaves (optional)

1. In a large saucepan cook pasta according to package directions; drain. Rinse with cold water; drain again. Transfer to a large bowl. Stir in tomatoes, cucumber, green onions, and olives.
2. For dressing, in a screw-top jar combine oil, lemon juice, basil, 2 tablespoons snipped or 2 teaspoons dried oregano, garlic, salt, and pepper. Cover and shake well. Drizzle dressing over pasta mixture; toss gently to coat. Transfer salad to a bowl or storage container; cover and chill overnight.
3. Tote salad, cheese, and, if desired, fresh oregano leaves in an insulated cooler with ice packs. Before serving, sprinkle salad with cheese. Garnish with oregano leaves. Makes 12 servings.

GREEK PASTA SALAD

Easy Does It
chill out

▼ Strawberry Rhubarb Lemonade

In a saucepan, combine 4 cups water, 2½ cups chopped fresh rhubarb, 1¼ cups sugar, and 1 tablespoon finely shredded lemon peel. Bring to boiling; reduce heat. Simmer, covered, 10 minutes. Remove from heat. Add 1 cup quartered fresh strawberries. Cool for 20 minutes. Strain through a fine-mesh sieve into a large pitcher. Stir 1 cup freshly squeezed lemon juice and 1 teaspoon vanilla into juice. Cool for 30 minutes. Cover and chill for 2 to 24 hours. Just before serving, add 1 cup fresh strawberries and lemon slices. Serve in ice-filled glasses. Makes 6 (1-cup) servings.

▲ Herb-Infused Lemonade

In an extra-large pitcher combine 12 cups cold water; two 12-ounce cans frozen lemonade concentrate, thawed; ⅓ cup sugar; and ¼ cup fresh lime juice. Combine well. Stir in torn fresh herb (tarragon, basil, or mint). Cover; chill for 8 hours. Strain through a fine-mesh sieve; discard herb. Cover and chill for up to 3 days. Serve over ice with fresh herb sprigs. Makes about 12 (1-cup) servings.

Raspberry Lemonade Spritzers

Place one 12-ounce package thawed frozen raspberries in a blender or food processor. Cover and blend or process until smooth. Press puree through a fine-mesh sieve to strain out seeds; discard seeds. In a punch bowl combine raspberry puree, 10 cups chilled sparkling water, and one 12-ounce can frozen lemonade concentrate, thawed. Serve in glasses over ice. Garnish with lemon slices and/or fresh raspberries. Makes 12 (1-cup) servings.

Madelines Lemonade

In a 2-quart pitcher combine 2 cups water, 1½ cups fresh lemon juice (6 lemons), 1 cup sugar, and ⅓ cup fresh lime juice (2 limes). Stir to dissolve sugar. Add 1 cup fresh raspberries. Cover; chill overnight. Serve over ice. Makes 8 to 9 (1-cup) servings.

Picnic Lemonade

Juice 12 lemons for about 3 cups juice. In a saucepan heat lemon juice and 1¼ to 1½ cups sugar until completely dissolved. Cool. In a 1-gallon container combine lemon juice mixture and 3 quarts cold water. Cover; chill until serving time. Serve in ice-filled glasses. If desired, add sprigs of fresh mint and lemon slices. Makes 12 to 14 (1-cup) servings.

summer

Make summer days
some of the best of
the year with these
wondrous get-together
and decorating ideas that
are as fun and fresh
as the season itself.

Wedding Shower Bliss

Fluffy cake, champagne toasts, and pretty decorations. There's a lot to love about this go-all-out bridal shower.

Take the Cake
The star of this festive cake is the topper: balloon-like macaroon pops. Just use purchased cookies and lollipop sticks. Snippets of ribbon add the final TA-DA!

Round and About

Balloons are always a sign that something special is going on. Honor the bride-to-be with large round helium-filled balloons in a crisp two-tone palette. Tie pretty silk ribbon tails to each and weight down by tying them to small river rocks.

Better Bubbles

Flavored syrup turns plain champagne into a signature cocktail. Offer guests lavender or ginger as festive stir-ins. Other champagne companions guests will raise a glass to include brandy-soaked pomegranate seeds, cranberry juice, citrus punch, and peach puree.

The Right Notes

When the invitations are sent, ask guests to RSVP with a song that reminds them of the bride-to-be. Make a playlist using the songs your guests suggest and record each one for the perfect custom music CD for the guest of honor.

Macaroon Pops

To offer guests more cookies on sticks, plant the pops in a sea of white candies. When the cookies are gone, pass the glass container around so everyone can get an extra handful of sweet indulgence.

Ring of Posies

Elegantly wrapped napkins dress up a bridal luncheon in a jiffy. To make these corsage collars, gather little posies of flowers and herbs then wrap the stems with ribbon. Cut a strip of paper about 7 inches long, notch the ends, and cut two slits about an inch from each end. Slip the posy stem through the slits to hold in place.

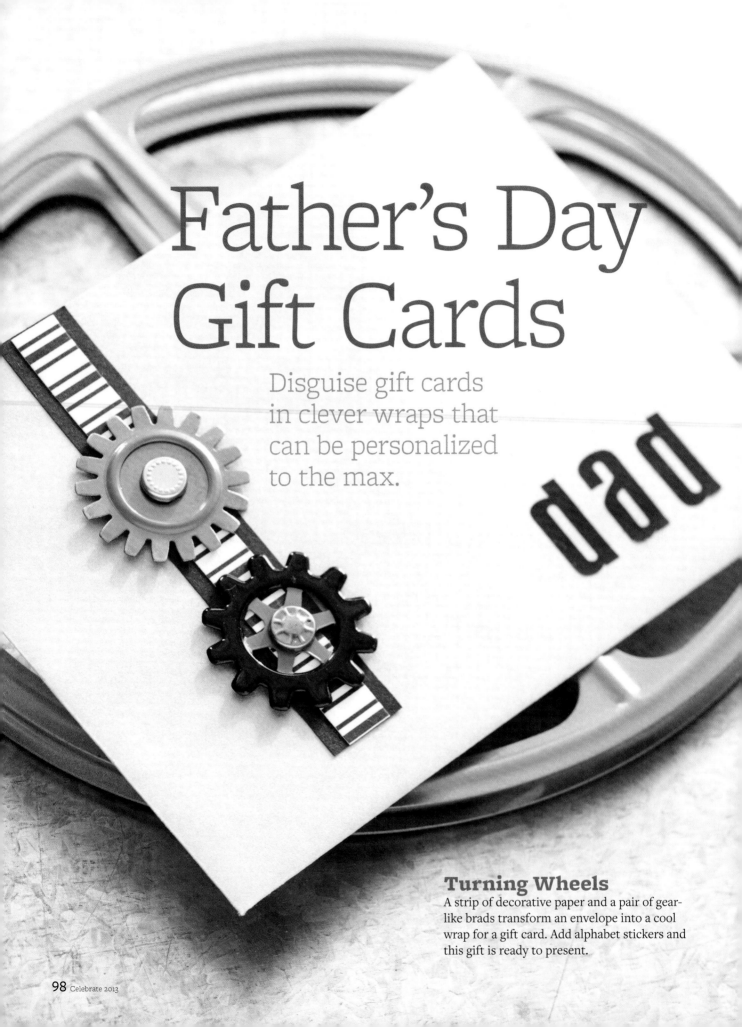

Father's Day Gift Cards

Disguise gift cards in clever wraps that can be personalized to the max.

dad

Turning Wheels

A strip of decorative paper and a pair of gear-like brads transform an envelope into a cool wrap for a gift card. Add alphabet stickers and this gift is ready to present.

Dad's Favorite Things

With dimensional stickers available in almost any theme, you're sure to find one to showcase things dad loves. Wrap a gift card in a small box and hot-glue ribbon in a T-formation, allowing room for stickers. Press the cutouts in place for a special wrap dad will long appreciate.

Bank on It

When dad's favorite spot doesn't offer gift cards, this makes a great substitute. On paper, write the name of the establishment where you'd like to take dad or where he'd like to shop. Then tuck in play or real money along with the note and he'll be thrilled at your thoughtfulness.

In with Tin

Choose a large dimensional sticker that coordinates with the gift card. Adhere it to the lid of a gift card tin for an extra-special wrap.

Mug of Fun

Dad will love this initial mug all by itself. But when he finds a gift card nestled inside a bag of crinkle shred, you'll really make his day top notch.

Picture Perfect

Combine a gift card with scrapbooking trims to make a clever mini collage. Create it to fit into a small frame and tie with a ribbon. Lucky dad, two gifts in one!

Fun by the Quart

A new quart paint can makes a masculine gift card holder. To add a handle, drill a hole in the center of the lid and attach a knob. To make the sleeve, cut scrapbook paper to wrap around the can and use double-sided tape to secure the edges. Metal scrapbooking tags draped from ball chain personalize the gift wrap.

Leaf of the Party

Set the scene for an outdoor party with accents gathered from the garden.

Table Topping

Instead of using a traditional cloth, look to the garden when setting your table. Place a runner of varied hosta leaves down the center, angling the foliage into a graceful line. Magnolia leaves also work well; both stay fresh for days without water.

It's a Cinch

A strand of big-leaf periwinkle is the most natural of napkin rings. This fast-growing vine is flexible enough to twist into a circle. Other supple vines to try are the young tips of bird's foot ivy clematis, morning glory, and sweet pea.

Coasting Along

Perfect for a garden party, large caladium leaves make fitting coasters. Other good options include hosta, magnolia, or maple-like leaves of viburnum opulus.

Garden Gathering

Collect nosegays in a basket at the gate or front door so each guest may take one home.

July 4th Salute

When Independence Day is near, accents in red, white, and blue fit right in.

Yard Star

A large metal star made to hang on a wall gets new life as a patriotic yard ornament. To cover each spoke, fold five different scrapbook papers in half and align each crease with the center of each spoke. Fold paper at spoke edges; cut out. Working on one spoke at a time, brush decoupage medium on the spoke and carefully press paper onto it. Repeat for each spoke. To cover seams and add a finished edge, hot-glue wide rickrack to outline each spoke.

Serve It Up

A flea-market wood tray is just the ticket for serving up something cold on the 4th of July. Sand any rough spots on the wood and wipe with a tack cloth. In a well-ventilated work area, spray the tray with red paint and let dry. Use a piece of scrapbook paper in patriotic colors to line the tray as desired. To make the liner waterproof, laminate it at a print shop and trim just beyond the paper edge. Use double-sided tape to adhere the liner to the tray center.

Party Smarts

Get kids excited about the new school year with an afternoon of fun and snacks.

Give a Hoot

Owl-print wrapping paper blankets the table with cute characters. If you can't find it, try stamping your own on crafts paper using different colors of ink. An owl figurine, often available in crafts and party supply stores, makes a handsome centerpiece. Shape a party hat for the fellow from patterned paper and top with a fringed tuft of tissue paper. Rubber stamps and wooden letters spell out words fitting for the theme.

Goodies to Go

Let kids pick their favorite color of take-home box brimming with fun school and art supplies. Natural color paper shred resembles noodles while a pair of pencils gives the look of chop sticks.

Smart Sips

Dress up individual-size milk bottles with a strip of decorative paper and press-on letters. Serve the good-for-you drinks with colorful straws.

Clipboard Snack Tray

Kids will love getting their very own clipboard to take home. Set the table using the boards as snack trays, clipping napkins in place.

Hootie Cuties

This parliament is an adorable clan. To make the owl cookies, use a stiff sugar cookie recipe for stick cookies. Use an egg-shape cookie cutter for body, a small oval for front, a pair of mini flowers for eyes, and a tiny triangle for the beak. Bake pieces separately, with the stick in the egg shape; let cool. Using the photo for inspiration, frost the large egg shape and place the small oval on top; frost the oval and sprinkle with baking candies. Add the flower shape eyes, adding frosting behind them. Frost eye centers with white and press a large flat candy dot in each center. Add the beak, frosting it yellow. Tie the top of each stick with strands of raffia. To display, wrap a plastic foam wreath with crepe paper and carefully press the sticks into the foam.

Chalk Talk

Craft place cards that resemble mini chalkboards. Use precut basswood rectangles, black mini canvases, and a strip of scrapbook paper. Hot-glue the canvas to the basswood 1 inch from the bottom edge. Use decoupage medium to adhere the paper strip below the canvas. Write each guest's name in white pencil on the canvas. Use a small wooden easel to hold the place card.

Taking Note

New school supplies always start the year off right. Arm each partygoer with a new tablet and set of pencils. To coordinate them with the decorations, purchase coverless tablets and use double-sided tape to adhere a decorative paper strip over the binding. For clever pencil presentation, slip a pair into woven finger traps.

Words to Remember

Encourage party guests to practice spelling with a quick, easy-to-do craft. Have them layer pretty paper strips with a slightly smaller piece of vellum, adhered at one end with a piece of double-sided tape or a staple. Use adhesive letters to spell out inspiring words. Make the strips long enough, and the little works of art can be used as bookmarks.

This easy-to-make photo booklet is a card and frame in one. Fold it flat for mailing, unfurl it for display. To make one, cut an 8½×11-inch sheet of patterned card stock in half lengthwise. Tape the narrow ends together to make one long strip. Accordion-fold the strip every 4 inches. Center a photo in each of the five squares, attaching with photo corners. Punch a hole in the back and thread with a ribbon tie. If desired, thread on a charm or two when tying closed.

Grandparents' Day Jubilee

Honor Grandma and Grandpa with hand-crafted tidbits filled with mug-shot love.

Paper Bouquet

Every grandparent loves photos of dear ones. To craft these handmade cards, add leaves and stems cut from green paper or felt to card stock. Create blooming frames using paper muffin liners with circular-cut photos glued to the centers.

Easy Does It
have a blast

▲ Fan Favors and Party Pops

Paper fans help guests keep cool. Insert sturdy straws or dowels between the ends of opened mini decorative paper fans (available at party supply stores; look for fans intended to hang by a string). Glue a circle of firework-patterned paper to the center. To call attention to drinks, print a label and glue it to holiday-theme paper cut in a rocket shape. Attach to a straw.

Ring ▶ Around the Sparklers

For festive party favors, lay sparkler boxes on white napkins and tie with napkin holders. Attach one end of a 12-inch length of grosgrain ribbon to the flat side of a D-ring (available at crafts and fabric stores); glue to secure. Loop around napkin and sparklers.

◄ Flare Chairs

Fire up chair backs with cloth-napkin covers. Fold a napkin in half; press to crease. Cut four pieces of ribbon; glue one inside each napkin corner. Tie to close. Hot-glue red cording to spell "4th." Short cording pieces become firework bursts.

▼ Lunch Pail

Paper rockets take off from a shiny sand-filled bucket. To make a rocket, roll scrapbooking paper into a tube; secure with glue. For the nose cone, cut a slit to the center of a paper circle; overlap and glue ends to form a cone. Glue a ribbon strip inside the rocket to resemble a fuse, and a long dowel opposite the ribbon.

▲ Lantern Love

Have a ball with round paper lanterns. Draw firework showers with red and blue marking pens on 12-inch white lanterns.

boo

Halloween Surprises

Get in the spirit of the haunting season with daring decorations and fiendishly good foods leading the way.

Cool Characters

Covered, carved, or cleverly painted, these pumpkins are oodles of fun to make!

No Fair Peeking

A little creepy, a little silly, this mummified white pumpkin comes alive as night falls. To make him, cut a lid into a white pumpkin and scoop out the insides. Carve out an egg-size oval for one eye. Use an apple corer to cut second eye. Press the cutout onto a toothpick; press into left eye opening to resemble a pupil. Cut two teardrop-shape nostrils along with a toothy grin. Slip turned-on battery-operated candles through pumpkin opening. Loosely wrap the carved pumpkin with gauze. To give an aged appearance, dampen a tea bag and blot it onto the gauze. If using real candles, do not use gauze.

Whooooo's Watching

This wide-eyed fellow is a welcome addition all autumn long. To make him, choose a pair of white lumpy gourds of similar size for eyes. Cut top off pumpkin and scoop out insides. Cut holes in pumpkin large enough to fit gourds, leaving approximately 1½ inches between holes. Carve zigzag edges. Cut a triangular beak and two ears from the pumpkin cutouts; slice off rind. For feathers, use an apple corer to cut and lift rind as shown. Pin ears and beak in place. Press eyes into sockets using toothpicks on inside to hold in place.

Unlikely Friends

This no-carve duo makes a pretty cute pair.

WHAT YOU'LL NEED

1 large and 2 small pumpkins
   (or a gourd for mouse)
2 round-head upholstery tacks
hammer; paintbrush
dark gray metallic acrylic paint
toothpicks and short wooden
   skewers sharpened on both ends
light gray acrylic paint
tracing paper
pencil; scissors
white card stock
thin-tip black marking pen
hot-glue gun and glue sticks
2 flat green marbles
paring knife
white crafts wire; wire cutters
ice pick
2 black quilting pins
wide orange ribbon

WHAT YOU DO

1. For the cat, choose a large pumpkin with a long stem to resemble a tail. Select a smaller pumpkin without a stem for the head. For nose, hammer an upholstery tack in the bottom center of the small pumpkin. Paint the pumpkins and tack with dark gray metallic paint; let dry.

2. Place the cat head and attach to body pumpkin with toothpicks and short wooden skewers.

3. For the mouse, choose a small pumpkin or oval gourd with a long stem. For nose, hammer in an upholstery tack in the bottom center of the pumpkin or gourd; paint it all light gray; let dry.

4. Trace the patterns on page 155; cut out. Cut two square cat ears and use patterns to cut grin, cat eyes, and mouse ears from white card stock. On the grin, draw in teeth with a thin-tip black marking pen. Hot-glue a flat green marble on each eye, draw a vertical line on each eye.

5. Paint ears a mixture of both gray paints to shade; let dry.

6. Use the paring knife to cut slits into pumpkins for ears. Carefully poke ears into place.

7. For cat whiskers, cut four pieces of wire, each 8 inches long. Randomly bend each piece into a zigzag. Poke two holes on each side of pumpkin center using an ice pick. Bend ends as needed and press wires into holes, securing with hot glue if needed.

8. For mouse whiskers, poke two holes on each side of pumpkin center using an ice pick. Press wires into holes, securing with hot glue if needed. Paint the whiskers using both gray paints; let paint dry.

9. Push in pins for mouse eyes. Tie ribbon around cat.

Boo Cat

Coloring books are great places to find carving inspiration such as this cat. Choose a pattern with a simple outline and few details. Trace it onto the pumpkin, adding a message if desired. Cut a lid, remove, and scoop out the pumpkin insides. Carefully carve along the lines, remembering to only carve out the negative spaces that are to be removed. Place a candle inside the carved pumpkin to illuminate the design. Do not leave burning candles unattended.

Black, White, and

Laden the table with black and white and pops of bright red. Mix and match patterns for a lively effect. For a large table or to create a pathway to the dining area, landscape with white pumpkins or paint traditional pumpkins black.

Set the stage for ghoulish gatherings with accents of red against black and white.

Red All Over

Drop-Dead Gorgeous

Plastic foam skulls center the table. Arrange a duo on a silver platter, raising one from the surface by taping it to a heavy candleholder. Dress up the tall fellow with a silver glittered top hat trimmed with red ribbon, adhesive gems, and large black and white crafts store feathers. Plastic glasses add sophistication.

Cameo Appearance

Thread a cameo charm onto red ribbon and tie around a monogrammed cloth napkin. To add black and white pattern to each place, choose cost-efficient paper dessert plates and layer on black or white dinner plates.

Take One If You Dare

Offer guests a variety of sweet concoctions from a new plastic organizer that's made to hold makeup. For small candies, such as cinnamon drops, pour them in plastic tubes, adding a candy eye, found in grocery stores with baking decorations, at the top of each. Place some candies in a pedestal bowl, inviting a few gummy worms to wiggle their way into the dish.

Soft Spot

If chair size allows, prop a black and white pillow on each to cozy up seating. Check discount stores for any black and white pattern to coordinate with the theme. Pillows can match or vary. For Halloween, anything goes!

Name That Ghoul

Back black and white print paper with solid black and add a strip of white for labeling. For a quick place card holder, use an office clip, slipping the paper between the wires.

Brew for You

Arrange bottles and a carafe on a silver tray for elegant presentation. A few drops of red food coloring turns a clear drink, even water, into a Halloween delight. Use silly straws for added fun.

Taking Shape

A shadowy glow burns softly behind Halloween silhouettes. Attach a variety of black die-cut figures to the outside of each hurricane lamp using double-stick tape. Place orange vellum paper over the cutouts and secure edges with vellum tape, which becomes invisible when the lanterns are lit.

Light the Night

Candlelight provides a flickering glow while still keeping the yard dark enough for frightful fun.

Star Struck

Light the way with a path of bright luminaries dressed for the occasion with stars punched from adhesive black paper.

Glowing Miniatures

Light up the night Halloween-style with orange and black luminaries.

WHAT YOU'LL NEED
tracing paper
permanent marking pen
clean empty cans
hammer and large nail
spray paint in orange and black
wire
tea-light candles

WHAT YOU DO

1. Draw simple bat, jack-o'-lantern, or Halloween motifs onto a clean can; trace with a permanent marking pen.

2. Fill the can with water; place it in the freezer. When the water in the can is frozen, remove it from the freezer.

3. Use a hammer and nail to puncture the design in the can. For a handle, punch two holes on opposite sides in the rim of the can, centering the design between the holes. Let the ice melt; allow the can to dry completely.

4. Cut a 16-inch length of wire. For handle insert one end of the wire into a hole near rim; twist the end of the wire into a loop. Insert the other wire end through the opposite hole, securing in the same manner.

5. Spray-paint the can orange or black. Let the paint dry. Place a tea-light candle inside each of the cans and hang securely from a branch or garden hook.

Night Lights

Illuminate a spidery path with paper bag luminaries. Decorate white bags with spider rub-ons, stickers, or trims. Fill bags with about 3 inches of sand and place on stairs or along a walkway amid a scattering of pumpkins. Insert battery-operated votive candles, pushing them into the sand for stability.

MONSTER MASH SLUSHES
Recipe on page 132

EYEBALL QUICHE FEAST
Recipe on page 132

Spooky Treats
& Sweets

Scare up
some fun at
a Halloween
party with
delectable sips
and nibbles.

MONSTER MASH SLUSHES

Monster Mash Slushes

Prepare the slush for these frosty concoctions a day or two before your party. Then add the special touches just before your guests arrive.

PREP 20 minutes FREEZE overnight

1   orange
¼   medium honeydew melon, seeded, peeled, and cubed (3 cups)
⅔   cup tequila
½   cup orange liqueur
4   cups ice cubes
    Coarse sugar or black sea salt
1   16-ounce bottle lemon-lime carbonated beverage, chilled
2   to 3 tablespoons grenadine syrup

1. Cut orange in half. Cut one half into wedges; wrap and chill overnight. Juice the remaining half; set juice aside.
2. In a blender combine honeydew melon, tequila, orange liqueur, and the reserved orange juice; cover and blend until smooth. With blender running, add ice cubes, a few at a time, blending until mixture becomes slushy. Pour into a 2-quart freezer container. Cover; freeze overnight.
3. To serve, rub the reserved orange wedges around rims of eight glasses. Dip rims in coarse sugar or black sea salt to coat; set aside. Using a heavy spoon, scrape frozen slush; scoop into prepared glasses. Add ¼ cup of the chilled lemon-lime beverage to each glass. Drizzle with grenadine. Makes 8 (8-ounce) servings.

Eyeball Quiche Feast

Our spooky quiche tartlets are decked out with olives, which double as eyes that watch guests wherever they go. Pictured on page 131.

PREP 50 minutes BAKE 20 minutes
COOL 10 minutes CHILL 1 hour
OVEN 375°F

1   recipe Pastry Dough
20 pearl onions or frozen pearl onions, thawed and halved
3   eggs
1½ cups whole milk
4   ounces Swiss or Fontina cheese, shredded (1 cup)
3   green onions, sliced
¼   teaspoon salt
¼   teaspoon ground black pepper
½   cup pimiento-stuffed green olives and/or large pitted black olives, sliced

1. Prepare and chill Pastry Dough. If using fresh pearl onions, place them in a saucepan of boiling water. Remove saucepan from heat and let stand for 5 minutes. Drain. When cool enough to handle, remove skins from onions; halve onions. Set aside.
2. Preheat oven to 375°F. Divide chilled Pastry Dough into 20 portions; shape each portion into a ball. Place one ball in each of twenty 2½-inch muffin cups. Press dough into bottoms and up sides of muffin cups. Set aside.
3. In a medium bowl beat eggs with a fork until well combined. Stir in milk, cheese, green onions, salt, and pepper. Ladle egg mixture into pastry-lined cups, filling each three-fourths full. On top of egg mixture in each muffin cup, layer pairs of pearl onion halves and olive slices.
4. Bake for 20 to 25 minutes or until a knife inserted near centers comes out clean. Let cool in muffin cups for 10 minutes. Using a sharp knife, carefully loosen sides and remove from muffin cups; serve warm. Makes 20 mini quiches.
Pastry Dough: In a medium bowl combine 2 cups all-purpose flour and ½ teaspoon salt. Using a pastry cutter, cut in ¾ cup butter until mixture resembles coarse crumbs. Sprinkle 1 tablespoon ice water over part of the flour mixture; gently toss with a fork. Push moistened dough to the side of the bowl. Repeat moistening flour mixture, using 1 tablespoon ice water at a time, until all is moistened (4 to 6 tablespoons ice water total). Gather dough into a ball, kneading gently until it holds together. Wrap in plastic wrap and chill about 1 hour or until easy to handle.

Mr. Bones and Double Dips

START TO FINISH 30 minutes

1   cup bottled roasted red sweet peppers
1   canned chipotle pepper in adobo sauce
1   teaspoon chili powder
12 ounces reduced-fat cream cheese (Neufchâtel), softened
2   tablespoons lime juice
    Salt
    Ground black pepper
4   ounces light sour cream
1   avocado
2   slices bacon or turkey bacon, crisp-cooked and finely crumbled
2   tablespoons snipped fresh cilantro
½   to 1 teaspoon ground cumin
6   cups desired vegetables and condiments, such as celery sticks for legs, cauliflower florets for head, sugar snap pea pods for ribs, baby carrots for shoulders and arms, small red sweet peppers for chest, grape tomatoes for feet, pimiento-stuffed green olive slices for eyes and spine, additional celery sticks, half zucchini slices, and/or red sweet pepper pieces for dipping

1. For smoky red pepper dip, in a blender or food processor combine roasted red peppers, chipotle pepper, and chili powder. Cover and blend or process until smooth. Add 8 ounces of the cream cheese and 1 tablespoon of the lime juice; cover and blend or process until smooth. Season to taste with salt and black pepper. Transfer smoky red pepper dip to a serving bowl; cover and chill while preparing creamy avocado dip.
2. For creamy avocado dip, in a clean blender or food processor combine sour cream, the remaining 4 ounces cream cheese, and the remaining 1 tablespoon lime juice. Cover and blend or process until smooth. Transfer sour cream mixture to a serving bowl. Seed and peel avocado; place in a small bowl and mash with a fork. Stir into sour cream mixture. Stir in bacon, cilantro, and cumin. Season to taste with *salt* and *ground black pepper*. If desired, cover and chill for up to 1 hour before serving.
3. For veggie platter, in the center of a large serving platter create a skeleton shape with some of the fresh vegetables. Arrange extra vegetables around edge of platter. (If desired, you can arrange the veggie platter before preparing the dips; cover and chill for up to 4 hours.) Serve veggie platter with smoky red pepper dip and creamy avocado dip. Makes 12 servings (2 cups red pepper dip and 1½ cups avocado dip).

GHOSTLY SPIRITS

Ghostly Spirits

Playful white chocolate ghosts add a frightfully festive touch to cocktails made for grown-up goblins.

PREP **10 minutes** CHILL **2 to 24 hours**

1¼ cups whole milk
⅓ cup whipping cream
¼ cup sugar
2 teaspoons vanilla
¾ cup vodka
⅔ cup white chocolate liqueur
Ice cubes
Pressurized whipped cream
White chocolate shavings and/or
White Chocolate Ghosts* (optional)

1. In a small pitcher or glass measure combine milk, whipping cream, sugar, and vanilla, stirring until sugar is dissolved. Stir in vodka and liqueur. Cover and chill for 2 to 24 hours.

2. To serve, for each drink, put ice cubes into a cocktail shaker; add ⅓ to ½ cup of the milk mixture. Cover and shake; pour into glasses. Top with whipped cream. If desired, sprinkle with chocolate shavings and/or top with White Chocolate Ghosts.

***White Chocolate Ghosts:** Line a baking sheet with waxed paper; set aside. Coarsely chop white chocolate (about 2 ounces). Place in a small microwave-safe bowl. Microwave on 100 percent power (high) about 1 minute or just until melted and smooth, stirring every 20 seconds. Place melted chocolate in a small resealable plastic bag; seal bag. Use kitchen scissors to snip a very small corner off the bag. Pipe small ghost shapes on prepared baking sheet. Add 2 miniature semisweet chocolate pieces to each ghost for eyes. Let stand until chocolate is set. Peel off waxed paper. Makes 6 to 9 (about 4-ounce) servings.

Tangled Web Shakes

Spun sugar creates a beautiful web of glossy strands on caramel and chocolate shakes. Work carefully when drizzling the sugar because it will be extremely hot.

START TO FINISH **30 minutes**

Caramel ice cream topping
Dark chocolate ice cream topping
⅓ cup sugar
Coarse sea salt
6 cups vanilla ice cream
¾ cup milk
3 tablespoons caramel ice cream topping
3 tablespoons dark chocolate ice cream topping

TANGLED WEB SHAKES

1. Drizzle caramel topping in a zigzag design inside each of eight 5- to 6-ounce glasses. Drizzle chocolate ice cream topping into each glass. Arrange glasses on a tray; freeze until needed.

2. Butter a large piece of foil; set aside. In a large heavy skillet spread sugar in an even layer. Heat over medium-high heat until sugar begins to melt, shaking the skillet occasionally; do not stir. When the sugar begins to melt, reduce heat to medium-low and cook about 5 minutes more or until all of the sugar is melted and golden, gradually stirring with a wooden spoon. With a spoon, immediately drizzle melted sugar in eight circles (each about 3 inches in diameter) onto prepared foil, drizzling zigzags inside the circles to resemble webs. Quickly sprinkle each with salt.* Set aside.

3. Just before serving, in a blender combine half of the ice cream, half of the milk, half of the 3 tablespoons caramel topping, and half of the 3 tablespoons chocolate ice cream topping. Cover and blend until smooth, stopping to scrape down sides as needed. Pour ice cream mixture into four of the prepared glasses. Blend remaining ice cream, milk, caramel topping, and chocolate ice cream topping. Top each shake with one salted-caramel web. Makes 8 (4-ounce) servings.

***Test Kitchen Tip:** The sugar will harden quickly, so it is helpful if someone else sprinkles salt on the webs right after drizzling as you continue to drizzle the melted sugar.

Popcorn Cone

Plain white paper drinking cones become funnels of fun. Decorate cones with black jack-o'-lantern faces and strips of patterned paper or ribbon. Fill the cones with caramel corn for a sweet old-time treat.

Tricky Treats

Hurry, hurry! Step right up for fun Halloween surprises assembled the old-fashioned way.

Tin Pail Alley

Metal pails in orange and black hold jelly beans with a jack-o'-lantern sucker sitting at center. If dropping the little gifts into beggars'-night sacks, first slip the filled buckets into clear plastic bags and tie closed with ribbon.

Classic Combination

Apples covered in caramel, chocolate, and nuts or candy sprinkles are neatly arranged on a cake plate ready for the grabbing. Let trick-or-treaters select their favorite then slip it into a cupcake liner and a clear cellophane bag tied with curling ribbon.

Lollipop Stand

Fool trick-or-treaters into thinking you spent hours decorating lollipops when you simply wrapped pops in cellophane and added a downloadable motif or sticker to each. Nestle the lollipops in a clear glass container filled with white jelly beans to serve when the kids come knocking.

Grab a Tall One

Get your wonder drink right here! Bottles of orange soda become pumpkin juice with the addition of a personalized printed label wrapping the bottle. Jaunty ribbons top off the unexpected treat.

Who'd Like One

Slip off the wrappers from candy bars and replace with paper sleeves trimmed with crepe paper, ribbon strips, and a fashionable Halloween sticker.

Pumpkin Tricks

Tape off and spray-paint pumpkins with bold black horizontal or vertical stripes. On unpainted sections, write words or initials. An apple corer or drill cuts through the skin to carve out dots. If you want candlelight to shine through, first carve a lid and scoop out the insides.

Eerie Entries

This season, greet guests with holiday spirit—ghostly gourds cleverly decorating an entry.

Spooky Style

If your fall is all about anticipating Halloween fun, then create a door that sets the mood. The centerpiece is an eye-catching, life-size removable tree decal. Use old chairs, barrels, metal laundry tubs, pails, and more to corral pumpkins. Add a few faux ravens positioned as in midflight. Repeat the stripe and dot motif by draping matching fabrics on the ladder and over barrels and tubs.

Gourd Greetings

Just a little paint will transform fall produce into eerie apparitions. First cover gourds with acrylic spray varnish. Use acrylic crafts paints to create design. To hang each gourd, drill a small hole through the top of the neck and thread florist's wire through it. Finish the display with dried vines, bittersweet berries, and even an abandoned paper-wasp nest.

Bird Brain

So much for deep thought—this jack-o'-lantern has become the victim of birds looking for their next brain to pick. To get the look, place the lid slightly askew and perch the predators on and around the pumpkin. Then enjoy the fun as trick-or-treaters discover the zaniness on their way to your front door.

Simply Fall

Engulf the entry with natural finds, such as pumpkins, gourds, sticks, and leaves. A square wreath makes an unexpected appearance while old keys, attached with wire, enhance the look on pumpkin fronts.

Skeleton Crew

These guys don't need to worry about broken bones as they caper form porch to rooftop. Easy to pose and secure with nearly invisible fishing line, the plastic skeletons can withstand weather and hang out the entire season.

Not every Halloween celebration is ruled by black cats and flying bats. Here's a table setting that will make you fall in love with autumn entertaining—minus the creepy crawlies.

Bittersweet Romance

Natural Attraction

White pumpkins show off bittersweet berries to their best advantage. Wrap long vines two or three times around each medium-size pumpkin. Secure the ends with floral wire. To better preserve the color of bittersweet berries, place cut ends of stems in about 1 inch of water while the berries dry out over a few days.

Please Sit

Gorgeous colors of bittersweet beckon guests to their places at the table. Let the luscious orange tones set the stage for table coverings, decorating accents, even beverages.

Simply Put

A wooden bowl displays freshly cut bittersweet. Be sure to keep the berried branches out of the reach of children and pets.

Orange Glow

Glass votives, partially filled with bittersweet berries, add to the warm autumn mood. Be sure to keep the flame well above the bittersweet.

Clear Sphere

A clear glass ornament serves as both placeholder and party favor. Remove the metal top and tuck a few sprigs inside. Use a glass marker to write a guest's name. Replace the top, cover with orange tape, and attach a twine hanger.

Perfect Pair

A glass hurricane provides the perfect vessel for bright bittersweet. Include a fall branch to lend a colorful complement.

Color March

Vintage glass bottles catch the light beautifully in a windowsill. Showcase a few bittersweet sprigs in coordinating colored bottles.

Easy Does It
pumpkins

▼Berried
An artificial berry stem is elegant against an orange background. Poke the wire end near the pumpkin stem then shape sprig. Tie a velvet ribbon bow around the stem.

▲Whimsical
Top off pumpkins with odds and ends of ribbon or felt secured with upholstery tacks. Metallic embroidery threads make a thready bow.

Dated

Adhesive foam letters put a spell on pumpkins. Stack two minis, one with no stem and the other with a long one. Attach Halloween date along with a sprinkling of foam stars. Tie a ribbon bow on the stem.

Glistening

Adhesive scrapbook trims transform plain pumpkins into fancy accents in seconds. Press scroll glittered trims onto pumpkin surface, adding a few press-on gems around the design.

Beribboned

Dress up a pumpkin with coordinating ribbon tape and wired ribbon. Run ribbon tape vertically, using the pumpkin grooves as guides. For the crowning glory, pin a generous bow front and center.

Patterns

HEARTFELT DINING
page 14–15
Full-Size Pattern

LOVE NOTES
TAG
page 29
Full-Size Patterns
cut 1 each

LOVE NOTES
HEART TAG
page 29
Full-Size Patterns
cut 1 each

CAKE ALL AROUND
page 9
Full-Size Pattern

CAKE ALL AROUND
page 9
Full-Size Pattern

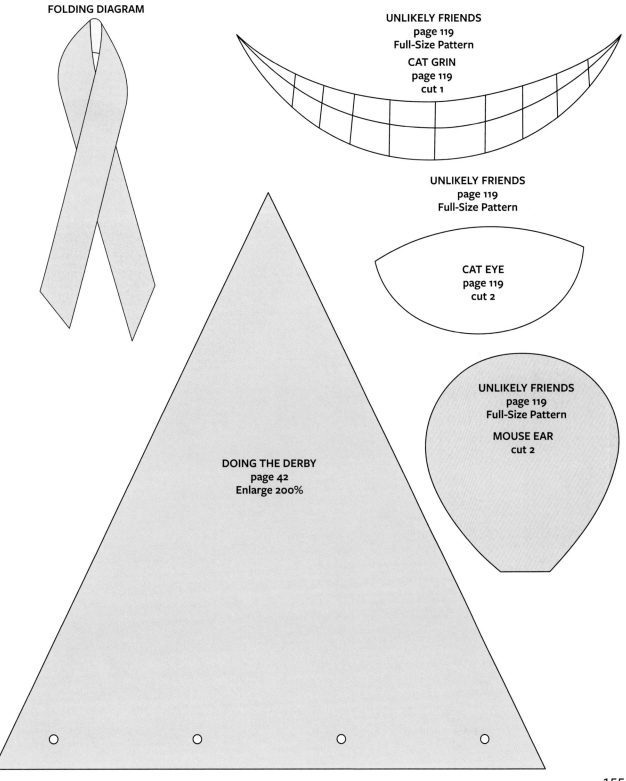

DOING THE DERBY PICTURE FRAME TRIM
page 45
Full-Size Pattern

FOLDING DIAGRAM

UNLIKELY FRIENDS
page 119
Full-Size Pattern

CAT GRIN
page 119
cut 1

UNLIKELY FRIENDS
page 119
Full-Size Pattern

CAT EYE
page 119
cut 2

UNLIKELY FRIENDS
page 119
Full-Size Pattern

MOUSE EAR
cut 2

DOING THE DERBY
page 42
Enlarge 200%

FAITH-FILLED WALL HANGING
page 61
Full-Size Lettering

FAITH-FILLED WALL HANGING
page 60-61
Enlarge 200%

FAITH-FILLED BOOKMARK
page 61
Full-Size Lettering

**FAITH-FILLED WALL HANGING
AND BOOKMARK**
page 61
Full-Size Template

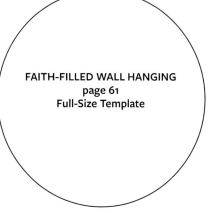

FAITH-FILLED WALL HANGING
page 61
Full-Size Template

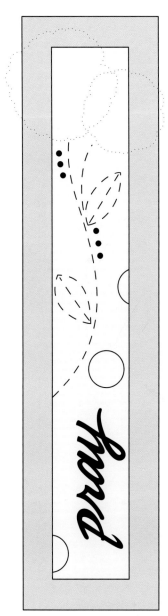

FAITH-FILLED BOOKMARK
page 61
Enlarge 200%

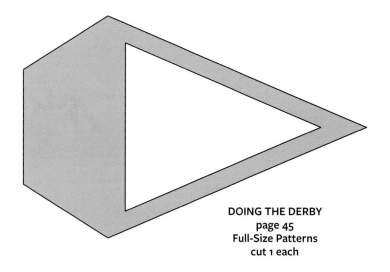

DOING THE DERBY
page 45
Full-Size Patterns
cut 1 each

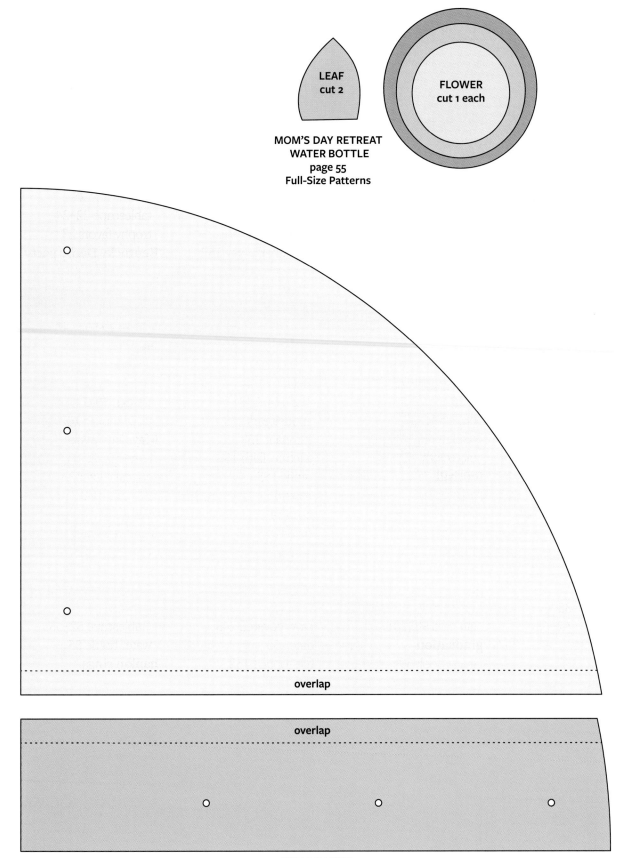

LEAF
cut 2

FLOWER
cut 1 each

**MOM'S DAY RETREAT
WATER BOTTLE**
page 55
Full-Size Patterns

overlap

overlap

**MAY DAY FUN
CANDY CONE**
page 41
Full-Size Patterns

Index

index *continued*

CREDITS & SOURCES
Photo Styling
Sue Banker and
  Catherine Brett
Photography
Jay Wilde

SOURCES
Pages 23, 25, 60–61, 62,
118–119, 140–141, 142:
Paint by Plaid Enterprises,
Inc., PO Box 7600,
Norcross, GA 30091-7600;
plaidonline.com.

Pages 63, 104: Decoupage
medium by Plaid
Enterprises, Inc.,
PO Box 7600, Norcross,
GA 30091-7600;
plaidonline.com.